In other times and places...
the person in transition left the village
and went into an unfamiliar stretch
of forest or desert.
There the person would remain for a time,
removed from the old connections,
bereft of the old identities,
and stripped of the old reality.
This was a time "between dreams"
in which fundamental chaos of the world's beginnings
welled up and obliterated all forms.
It was a place without a name—
an empty space in the world
and the lifetime where a new sense of self
could gestate.

—*William Bridges*
from Transitions: Making Sense of Life's Changes

Copyright © 2013 Imagine a World Publishing
The Time Between Dreams: How To Navigate Uncertainty in Your Life and Work

ISBN: 978-0-9881848-0-0
Library of Congress Control Number: 2012914773
10 9 8 7 6 5 4 3 2 1
Printed in the United States of America

Book design by Jane Jeszeck, Jigsaw | jigsawseattle.com
Editing by Sandy Marvinney
Cover design by CreateSpace, createspace.com
Back cover copy by Valory Reed, veedot.com
Indexing by Michael Ferreira, ferreiraindexing.com
Author, p. 99, p. 161 photographs by Dennis Williams, williamsphoto.com
Graphics from dreamstime.com: p.13 © Cienpies, pp.19, 20, 22 © Georgios, p.49 ©zenwae, p.56
    © Experimental, p.57 © Arkela, p.59 © Greg Epperson, p.72 © Xochicalco, p.76 © Epistock, p.78
    © Jpsdk, p. 87 © Atee83, p.142 Artenot, p.143 © Deduhin.

Centerpoint Institute for Life and Career Renewal has granted exclusive rights to Carol A. Vecchio
    for use of its copyrighted and trademarked materials (Natural Cycles of Change, LifeWork
    Renewal, Passion Search, Exploring Options), client stories, and graphics, centerpointseattle.org
"The Parable of the Trapeze" is from *Warriors of the Heart* by Danaan Parry, reprinted by permission
    of Earthstewards Publishing, earthstewards.org
Quotation from *Transitions: Making Sense of Life's Changes* by William Bridges, 2004,
    Second Edition, reprinted by permission of Susan Bridges, wmbridges.com
Quotations from *A Joseph Campbell Companion, Reflections on the Art Living* by Joseph Campbell,
    1991, reprinted by permission of the Joseph Campbell Foundation, jcf.org
Quotations from *The Power of Myth* by Joseph Campbell and Bill D. Moyers 1988 reprinted by
    permission of Random House, Inc.

Imagine a World Publishing
c/o Centerpoint Institute
4000 NE 41st Street
Seattle WA 98105
206.686.LIFE
centerpointseattle.org

The TIME BETWEEN DREAMS

How to Navigate Uncertainty *in Your* Life *and* Work

Carol A. Vecchio

Imagine a World Publishing
SEATTLE, WASHINGTON

TABLE OF CONTENTS

Right Places | Measuring Winter Activity | Loneliness into Solitude...
and the Second Phase of Winter | Passion Search | Dreaming Can
Be Scary | Planting Seeds of Vision | Mini-Transition(s) in Winter |
Renewal Point | Challenges That May Arise in Winter | Worksheet:
Times I've Been in Winter | Helpful Winter Activities | Spring Forward

*Dedicated to the community
of past and present Centerpoint clients and core faculty:
your courage to ask the difficult questions
and find your life's purpose
is the inspiration for, and the heart of,
this work.*

INTRODUCTION
Change Happens

WE'VE ALL HEARD THAT "change is the only thing in life that we can count on," but wouldn't life be so much easier if things would just stay the way they are right now?

Well, maybe not right at this particular moment. Perhaps you have picked up this book because you are feeling a bit confused about your life or your work. But how about those times when you felt that everything was going effortlessly, when you felt in the groove and wished you could make that one moment last a lifetime?

Stop a minute and imagine it ... What would it be like to feel that way day after day, year after year, decade after decade? No worries, no concerns, never feeling overwhelmed or stressed out, just living in a "happily ever after" world. Does it sound like heaven to you?

Well, I'm truly sorry to say that your life can't be like that—neither I nor anyone else throughout history has figured out how to accomplish it. Life is messy. Life is confusing. Life is uncertain.

> *Happiness is the lull between problems.*
> —Paul Reiser

Life is like riding a roller coaster in the dark—we are unaware of what is around the bend, how far up or down we have to travel on that track, or when it will feel as if the bottom has dropped out. We each have our own way of dealing with that uncertain ride: some look forward to the thrill of what will pop up and surprise them; some find themselves terrified, holding on and screaming the entire time; and some will stay as far away from that ride as possible.

What's your style? Are you the kind who jumps head first into the thrills; who, after the first ride can't wait to go find a new, more exciting experience? Maybe you are someone who would ride that same roller coaster over and over again until you could feel more comfortable knowing what's going to happen next? Or are you one to avoid the ride altogether because you get the jitters just glimpsing it?

The roller coaster is a simplistic metaphor for describing how we experience change in our lives. There are days when the idea of taking a risk and bounding right in would be fun, and other days when imagining all the energy it would take to even get to the ride keeps us safe at home. We each have different comfort levels with change, due to many different factors. We need to consider all parts of our lives and selves as we navigate uncertainty. Addressing just one, a career for example, is like planning in a vacuum. As we focus on career questions, we also need to deal with all the other aspects of life. Life is complicated.

Shifting Perspectives

The perspective throughout this book envisions life as an "inside out" process, valuing introspection and personal responsibility. Before taking any external action, we make each choice a conscious one. Those who make decisions the other way around from the "outside in" tend to be overly swayed by external influences like others' expectations of them and what they "should" do. I don't mean to imply all "shoulds" are bad; for example, we should treat each other with care and kindness. But how much more impactful that choice is when we know it's the right thing to do based on personal, prior experience and our own internal sense of right and wrong.

"Outside In" Approaches to the Job Search

As career counselors, we find our potential clients' first question is often, "Who's hiring?" or "What jobs are available?" A traditional approach to job hunting encourages us to learn about industries that are growing and then apply for opportunities in those fields. Will we be happy, fulfilled, or satisfied with that direction? Who knows? There's always a chance that one could get lucky and land a position that is a good fit. What are your odds of success? Well, let's just say that I wouldn't want to bet on that horse.

From the flip side, the first question that some career counselors will ask a new client is "What occupations have you been considering?" This question is not as helpful as it might first appear. People who expected to work hard and climb the ladder of success are in a world of hurt. *Fast Company* magazine calls it flux: the chaotic frontier of business.

> *Our institutions are out of date; the long career is dead;*
> *any quest for solid rules is pointless. ...*
> *you can't rely on an established business model*
> *or a corporate ladder to point your way.*

The world is changing faster than we can keep up; new occupations are perpetually invented. For example, technological changes occur exponentially. According to Ray Kurzweil, in the 21st century we won't simply experience 100 years of progress. At the rate we are moving now, it will be more like 20,000 years of progress in that time period. How to even keep track of the turbulence that this causes? If I explored what I can do career-wise based on the job titles I currently know about, then I would most certainly be limiting my options.

The Twenty-First Century Workplace

The pundits predict that the traditional job will go the way of the dinosaur. Instead, we will be working via assignments and projects. Research by the Human Capital Institute reveals that at least one-third of the U.S. workforce is now composed of freelancers, also known as contract workers. The pool of these workers, who often are part time, is growing at more than twice the rate of the full-time workforce. The Bureau of Labor Statistics states that from 1990 to 2008 the number of contract positions grew from 1.1 million to 2.3 million and included a larger share of workers in higher skill occupations. This means that the number of people freelancing more than doubled during that time period. There is every indication that this future trend will not stop or even slow down.

The workplace of the not-so-distant future won't provide many external benefits. Pensions, tenure, and even health insurance will be features of the past. As a matter of fact, in 1994 the percentage of "core positions" in the workforce—those with benefits—was 70 percent; by the year 2006, it had dropped to 40 percent.

We move from one opportunity to the next, finding opportunities by continuously uncovering, as Richard N. Bolles in *What Color is Your Parachute?* elaborates on Frederic Buechner's approach, "The intersection of what you love doing and what needs doing in the world." If each of us can define what we love—our WorkVision statement—then we can use that as a compass to find the place in the work world where we are needed most. Once that "intersection" is either accomplished or inevitably changes, then we will need to find a new one. This is a major shift in the way we view the job market. We have to define our path, follow our passions, and self-direct the process. In the future this will be our only option to navigating the labor force.

Shifting to an "Inside Out" Approach

Mark Savickas, a well-known career development theorist, expresses it this way: "It's not about fitting yourself into work, it's about finding out how work fits into your life." This inside out approach also entails examining more than just your career needs. It is a matter of clarifying how you want to balance your life—how you want to live your life overall. What roles do elements like family, community, creativity, work, personal growth, meaning, and environment play for you?

That's what this book is about. In the work that we've done at Centerpoint Institute for Life and Career Renewal over the past 20 years, we value the central role that change plays in our work, our lives, our communities, and our world and have developed a "map" that helps us navigate it more consciously and gracefully.

> *If your time to you*
> *Is worth savin'*
> *Then you better start swimmin'*
> *Or you'll sink like a stone*
> *For the times they are a-changin.'*
> —Bob Dylan, The Times They Are A-Changin,' 1963

Bob Dylan wrote these lyrics in the 1960s and they are just as relevant now as they were then. In the twenty-first century, we live in a society where technological advances have radically shifted the ways we work and we live. Now, more than ever, we have to start "swimmin'."

Roller coasters, swimmin'—it's ironic that I've used these images since I haven't set foot on a roller coaster in over 40 years and can barely swim! When I think of either one, I feel panicky and uncomfortable. A very similar reaction can arise when changes occur in our lives.

I have found in my own life, though, when I can face my fears, meet them head-on, and listen to what they have to teach me, I can then learn a little more about myself and grow into the person I am continually becoming.

I hope that this book will do the same for you. It will be applicable no matter what kind of changes you are experiencing or between what dreams you might find yourself. It will, I hope, inspire creativity, passion, and renewed commitment in many areas:

- **Individual:** when you find yourself at developmentally difficult periods in your life, be they career, personal, age- or health-related.

- **Relational:** if you are struggling with whether you want to remain in a relationship, job, church, club, geographical location, or assessing with whom to grow old—a mate, friends, professional colleagues, pets, family.

- **Spiritual:** if you are wondering if life can feel more meaningful/purposeful for you or addressing whether a belief system is too small, too big, or no longer resonates.

- **Financial:** if you are grappling with how to change jobs and meet your financial obligations or when to retire and with some financial security.

- **Corporate:** when businesses reorganize, merge, or reinvent themselves.

Our ideas about our careers, jobs, relationships, families, where we live, and even who we are, change over time. By acknowledging that such change is normal and natural, this book offers guidance for moving forward from what isn't exciting you to doing what will enliven you.

There are a number of topics that this book won't cover: how to uncover your passions, define your vision, conduct a job search, or advance in your career. It will help you understand how to navigate the uncertainty that accompanies deciding what you want. You will learn about what needs to be in place for you to achieve your next steps in whatever area of your life is changing.

The time between dreams describes those times over the course of our lives when we feel lost—when we know what we don't want but have no clue about how to define our future. It is during such phases of feeling adrift that we can gain the perspective, renewal, and space to heal our hearts and discover our purpose in life. In a more elemental way, the time between dreams can also be defined as each waking and precious day we have on this earth. Both are times we must cherish: only then can we live fully and consciously and be truly alive.

> *Happiness requires an ability to tolerate uncertainty.*
> —Gordon Livingston, MD

If you are ready to live from the "inside out" and learn how to successfully navigate change and uncertainty in every aspect of your life, you have found the right guidebook. Immerse yourself in its words, take time to complete the worksheets, and get ready to view your experiences from both a new, and an ancient, perspective.

How Change Happens:
A Linear Model vs. a Cyclical Approach

Trust that which gives you meaning and accept it as your guide.
—Carl Gustav Jung

IN OUR DAY-TO-DAY existence we are continually bombarded with strong messages that dictate what success is, how our lives are supposed to progress, and how to navigate change. If I were to draw a picture or visual of those messages, it might look like this:

A LINEAR APPROACH
And sound like this:
- Keep climbing the ladder, no matter what happens and at whatever cost.
- Always build upon what you've done in the past.
- Don't leave a job until you have another one in hand.
- Life is a constant upward and forward progression.
- Find that perfect [fill in the blank] and live "happily ever after."

We are also told that there is a "formula" that will keep us on this straight and narrow path. These popular maxims are familiar to everyone:

- Think positively.
- Set clear goals.
- Be persistent.
- Never give up.
- If it's to be, it's up to me!

In fact, all these maxims are helpful and good *some* of the time. What happens, though, when we find ourselves doing all to the utmost but we still feel like everything is falling to pieces around us? When, no matter how hard we work or how firm our willpower, we still don't get the results we seek?

We tend not to question the "formula" and its linear approach to life. Instead, we usually hurl criticisms back on ourselves: What's wrong with me? Why can't I be more productive and organized? Why is my life falling apart unlike everyone else's? They all seem to be humming along just fine!

A client, "Sanjay," scheduled an appointment with me. He was an attorney in a one of those mega-sized law firms and he was miserable. While he had only been practicing for two years, he felt like he was in the wrong career. He remarked that he looked around at everyone else in the office and he knew he was the *only* one who felt this way. Every single person appeared passionate and engaged. Since attorneys are one of my specialty areas and having assisted many over the past 30 years, I asked with which firm he worked. I was able to reassure him that he was, in fact, *not* the only one at his firm who was unhappy. Many people can portray an outwardly positive appearance while inside they are dying a slow death. We keep up appearances because we buy into the idea that we need to look successful to all those around us, at all times.

But inside we feel like a failure, beat ourselves up, and become our own worst enemy.

What if I were to say that we can look at our lives from a very different, and consequently, much more productive perspective? Instead of a linear model, let's consider a cyclical approach to how we live our lives, make choices, and move forward.

A Cyclical Approach, an Ancient Idea

A cyclical model allows room for ups *and* downs, for being out there *and* stepping back, for action *and* introspection. It's a much more organic approach versus a mechanical one.

This idea is not new. Ancient cultures, especially those in which people lived close to the land, understood the natural cycles of nature and applied that cyclical understanding to day-to-day life and the culture's rites of passage.

For example, a central tenet of many Native American cultures includes a medicine wheel, a symbol of the life journey that guides one on a path toward wholeness. It is circular, with spokes emanating from the center, and represents the unending cyclical nature of and the balance essential to life. Each quadrant (although some medicine wheels have six or more segments) delineates each of the four cardinal directions: north, south, east, and west. They are often symbolized by different colors and by animal totems. Different native tribes might represent the medicine wheel differently; what remains essentially similar is the idea that life is a circle and at the center is the eternal fire from which we gain healing, knowledge, and wisdom. Shannon Thunderbird, descendent of the "Originals," the Coast Tsimshian people in British Columbia, Canada, eloquently describes this process:

The Medicine Wheel has been adopted by most First Nations people as a universal symbol of healing, interconnectedness and a holistic foundation of peaceful interaction and personal growth … .

The "Old" People say that you are never the same person coming out of a circle as when you went in because so many new connections have been made. All things that live within the Sacred Hoop are equal and protected. It is a place where you come together in safety,

*trust and sanctity to share stories and feelings and help each other heal
through both communal and individual laughter and tears.
Eventually you will return to your starting place older
and hopefully a little wiser to begin the process of walking the Wheel again,
this time with new understanding, insight and inner strength.*

On the other side of the globe, the *yin yang* of Chinese culture with its familiar graphic takes a similar approach. It represents the intertwined duality and complexity of all things in nature. Harmony and balance are the fundamental ideas behind *yin yang*. While *yin* and *yang* are opposites, combined they create the whole. Nothing can exist without both and nothing is completely one or the other. It understands the necessity for paradoxes.

*To yield is to be preserved whole.
To be bent is to become straight.
To be empty is to be full . . .
To have little is to possess.*

—Lao Tzu, *Tao Te Ching,* Chapter 22, 3rd to 6th century BC

Cyclical symbols have existed throughout history and cultures, including medieval times. The Wheel of Fortune, or *Rota Fortunae*, belongs to the goddess Fortuna, who spins it at random and at her whim, changing the positions of those on the wheel: some suffer great misfortune, others gain windfalls.

*Fortune can, for her pleasure, fools advance,
And toss them on the wheels of Chance.*

—Juvenal, Roman poet, late 1ˢᵗ and early 2ⁿᵈ century AD

16

The wheel usually has four stages, represented by four humans. These stages, as described in *The Dictionary of the Middle Ages*, are as follows:

Regno: I reign. The figure at the top of the wheel, often portrayed with a crown.

Regnabo: I shall reign. The figure rising on the left side of the wheel.

Regnavi: I have reigned. The figure on the right side of the wheel, falling from grace.

Sum sine regno: I have no kingdom. The figure at the bottom of the wheel who has fallen completely out of Fortune's favor. This person is sometimes thrown completely from the wheel, or even crushed by it, with the belief that there is no chance to reign again.

I know how Fortune is ever most friendly and alluring
to those whom she strives to deceive, until she overwhelms them with grief
beyond bearing, by deserting them when least expected. ...
Are you trying to stay the force of her turning wheel? Ah! dull-witted mortal,
if Fortune begin to stay still, she is no longer Fortune.

—Boethius, The Consolation of Philosophy, 524 AD

From this extremely brief glimpse into a range of cultures throughout history, you can begin to see that this cyclical concept is universal and ancient. In psychology and in the human development fields, however, this idea is relatively new.

Cycles in Psychology

Carl Jung, a Swiss psychiatrist during the first 60 years of the twentieth century and founder of analytical psychology now also referred to as depth or humanistic psychology believed that life has a spiritual purpose beyond material goals. He tapped into this idea of cycles and proposed that our main task in life is to discover and fulfill our deep innate potential, like an acorn growing into an oak or a caterpillar becoming a butterfly.

Some of Jung's work also focused on mandalas. Loosely translated, the Sanskrit word mandala (*pronounced* MAHN-da-la) means "circle." For Jung, the mandala was a symbol of wholeness, completeness, and perfection, and symbolized the self.

One of Jung's own mandalas

Jung said that a mandala symbolizes "a safe refuge of inner reconciliation and wholeness" and is "a synthesis of distinctive elements in a unified scheme representing the basic nature of existence." Jung used the mandala as a tool for his own and his patients' personal growth.

Another tenet of Jung's work involved archetypes. If you've ever taken the Myers-Briggs Personality Type Indicator, then you already know something about Jung's typology. It outlines four major dichotomies—introversion/extraversion, intuiting/sensing, feeling/thinking, and perceiving/judging. (An interesting aside for us psychology geeks—the last category was added after Jung's death.) The combinations of these dichotomies allow for 16 different personality types from which to understand ourselves better. They provide a way to make Jung's theories applicable and useful.

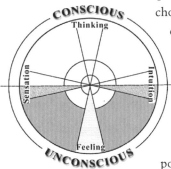

At left is a visual of how Jung, in 1925, delineated the archetypes in mandala form. He referred to it as a compass. Notice that the upper and outer portions of the circle represent the Conscious. Related to the Conscious is the next layer, Thinking. The lower, outer area is the Unconscious and connected to it, Feeling. On the right and left, Intuition and Sensation are mapped.

As you learn more about the Natural Cycles of Change model outlined in the upcoming chapters, you may want to revisit this brief history of medicine wheels, *yin yang*, Fortuna, and Jung's mandala and "compass" to deepen your understanding. All these paradigms are included in and are the foundation for a tool that you can use in daily life.

More recently in the 1960s, Yale psychologist Daniel J. Levinson developed a comprehensive theory of adult development by conducting a longitudinal study of the lives of men. (Yes, men; remember, this *was* the 1960s.) His book, *The Season's of a Man's Life*, outlined his findings. Some years later he also studied women's stages of development. Interestingly, he found similar patterns. You may be familiar with the more popular book at that time, *Passages* by Gail Sheehy, which drew on Levinson's study for its premises.

Levinson delineated two distinct phases in the adult years. He called one a life structure and the other transition. Each phase lasts for an average of five to ten years, so the seven-year itch concept with which we're familiar has a lot of basis in truth.

Centerpoint's Natural Cycles of Change

All the above studies and concepts, plus the more contemporary work of Frederic Hudson, who overlapped Levinson's phases on a cyclical representation in his book *The Adult Years,* form the conceptual basis for the Centerpoint Natural Cycles of Change model.

Let's outline its basic components: It begins with a **Cyclical Approach** in which every experience creates an opportunity for growth and renewal during which we manage two distinct periods of time: the first, using Levinson's terminology, is a **Life Structure.**

In a **Life Structure,** while changes may be occurring in our lives, we have a fit with our external world and predominantly feel a sense of stability.

life structure

life transition

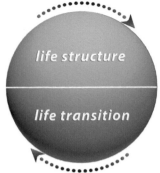

life structure

life transition

This period alternates with a **Life Transition** during which we face much uncertainty and change in our lives. We have no clear sense of our place or fit in the world. "Alternates" is a key word here. The movement from Structure to Transition and back again happens in a normal, alternating pattern throughout the adult years.

At this point we may be reminded of the concept of the mid-life crisis. Oh yes, this is definitely part of our adult experience! However, remember the seven-year itch concept? On average we will experience this shift from life structure to life transition more frequently than just in midlife.

Development Stages

Levinson identified five main stages delineated by ages, which he called eras, in the lives of those he studied.

Preadulthood (birth to age 22)

Early adulthood (age 17 to 45)

Middle adulthood (age 40 to 64)

Late adulthood (age 60 to 85)

Late late adulthood (age 80 and over)

These stages overlap because human beings never seem to fit into neat, specific boxes, even though that would make life so much more predictable. Levinson divided the adult stages into subcategories to analyze them further. He found that periods for building (stability) consistently alternated with times for questioning (transition). The stages he identified can be described on the table on the following page.

While Levinson was quite specific in outlining the eras as connected to age, in our work at Centerpoint we have learned to use these delineations as a broad, general guideline. They do not unfold in the same way for everyone, but relate to what we are learning and how we are growing at a particular time. Some people may chronologically fall into the "late adulthood" stage but, because of their particular life circumstances, have never experienced a major life transition. It's tough to face your first big shift at age 60. So while the stages may have some correlation with age, our personal journeys may not match up exactly with Levinson's eras because each person is a unique being.

CYCLE	STAGE	AGE	MAIN ACTIVITIES
Transition	Early adult transition	17–22	Step out into the world and explore life.
Stability	Enter adult world	22–28	Start a family and pursue a dream.
Transition	Age 30 transition	28–30	See flaws in the plan and reevaluate or more clearly define the dream.
Stability	Settle down	33–40	Concentrate on family/community connections and strive to achieve newly honed dream.
Transition	Midlife transition	40–45	Question major areas of life; this transition may feel like a crisis.
Stability	Enter middle adulthood	45–50	Create a new life structure, which might include a new job/career; explore other areas such as recreation, graduate school.
Transition	Age 50 transition	50–55	Reevaluate again; crisis may be possible, especially if none occurred during the midlife transition.
Stability	Culmination of middle adulthood	55–60	Satisfying era (similar to earlier settle down stage) if one has adjusted to prior changes.
Transition	Late adult transition	60–65	Prepare for retirement; major turning point.
Stability	Late adulthood	65 +	Create new life structure for retirement and aging; prepare for physical decline.

Additionally, because of how fast the world has been evolving and changing over the past 50 years, I'm not sure that many of us would define the ages between 22 and 28 as "stable." How many people do you know in that age group who are settling down to start families and pursue their dreams? Many people in their twenties still live at home with their parents. New developmental stages have been delineated with three distinct phases to adolescence: early, middle, and late. Add in the "quarter-life crisis" (analogous to the mid-life crisis) occurring during one's twenties and early thirties and you experience many transitions all before the age of 35.

Changes have occurred at the other end of the spectrum as well. With the populace living longer, the transition to retirement is occurring later than the early sixties in many cases, especially given the economic destabilization we have experienced. People in this age category either feel ready to use their wisdom and experience to make a bigger difference, or they are not financially able to retire. Enter Marc Freedman and the idea of "encore careers" and "rehirement." Yes, the stages of life are becoming much more complicated than ever before.

The Foundation of the Cycle

The **Life Structure** and **Life Transition** aspects of the cycle relate to our identity in the world, i.e., who am I as I achieve and create things in the world and who I am apart from my external identities? Or, in connecting the dots back to our earlier discussion, we can understand Life Structure and Life Transition to Fortuna's stages of "I reign," I'm on top of the world, and "I have no kingdom," I'm crushed under the wheel of fortune, or to Jung's dichotomies of Conscious (Thinking) and Unconscious (Feeling).

Next, if we draw a line vertically on the circle, it shows that we move from *transition* toward *structure*, from uncertainty toward stability in whatever aspect of life is changing. Another way to word this is that we are ready to shift the focus from the internal to the external.

On this side of the cycle:

1. We have a clear vision, dream, or goal for what we want, and

2. We have the energy to make that vision a reality.

With our vision clear and energy abundant, our activity is focused outwardly; we step into the world to launch and build our dreams.

On the other side of the cycle, we move from structure toward transition, from stability toward uncertainty and change. We travel from the external to the internal. Again, two factors influence this side but now:

1. We have no clear direction or vision for the future, and

2. We have less energy and find it difficult to accomplish anything significant.

We must focus our activity inwardly so we can step back and step in to find a new vision.

The Essential Nature of Energy

We all know at least a few people who thrive on ideas; we often refer to them as visionaries. Ideas for these folks are like oxygen—a basic and vital necessity. When you ask them "What do you want to do next?" they can verbalize a multitude of possibilities. If they are on the left side of the circle, they have the energy to go out and climb great mountains. If, however, they find themselves with little energy available, no matter how many ideas they might have, none will come to fruition. They are confused because they think they should be able to make some happen. But if there is no available energy even the best ideas will lay fallow; they simply aren't able to follow through.

Not "Either/Or" But "Both/And"

Another way to think about these two sides of the cycle is in terms of "doing" and "being." My husband sometimes calls himself a "human doing" instead of a human being. He says if he's not engaged in some activity he feels unproductive and lazy. We often value the outer more than the inner. When we look at matters cyclically, though, both are essential. We can't have one without the other.

Still, many people don't understand the need for both. Not long ago I read a newspaper article about a trend in newly published books. In the recent past, book subjects have been focused on messages such as *just do it, go for it, take action.* The article talked about a new genre of titles focused around just the opposite: *slowing down, relaxing, and the virtue of not doing.* As the author was contrasting these two seemingly opposing perspectives, I found myself getting more and more frustrated. Why must we choose one over the other? At the heart of a cyclical approach is the understanding that we need both! There are times for making things happen and times for stepping back. While many people would have us believe that one was better than the other, I contend that this isn't an "either—or" situation. We need it all: activity *and* rest, doing *and* being, our inner *and* outer existences, *yin yang.*

> Through pride we are ever deceiving ourselves. But deep down below the surface of the average conscience a still, small voice says to us, something is out of tune.
>
> ~Carl Jung

Step In and Step Out

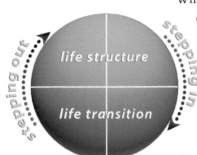

When we view life from a cyclical perspective, we allow ourselves periods for growth *and* renewal. If we think about it, these cycles of life are familiar to us. We engage in them daily and weekly. Anytime we make a decision, on some level, we check in with ourselves. Sometimes it happens so quickly and intuitively that we don't even notice that step. Often, though, we make more conscious choices.

I've always had this interesting relationship with food. Growing up in an Italian-American household, the word I heard most was *Mangia! (Eat!)* I was always encouraged to clean my plate and eat everything on it; on special occasions that meant an over-abundance of everything. I have had to learn how to know when I was full and be able to say "No more." When I'm hungry, instead of going to the fridge and looking for something to eat, I have practiced a different approach. I first check in with myself to find out what I'm craving and what I need. Then I can search that out and then feel more satisfied. Many people can do that without thinking; I've had to make it a conscious process.

When we introduced this cyclical idea to the graphic artists who developed Centerpoint's first logo so that they could incorporate it into their design, the first thing they said was "Oh, that's the life of a project." It described the way they worked with their clients. First they would listen to the client's needs and then step back to play around with ideas that might fit. Sometimes it took a while, but when they hit on a design that had a lot of energy and excited them, they would meet with the client and make their pitch. The client would love it so they closed that deal and started the process all over again with the next project. Their work is, in effect, a creative cycle.

In terms of human physiology, we can think about our need for activity and rest—the hours of the day when we are active and those when we must sleep. Even more basic is our need to breathe. We take oxygen in and then let it out. If we only did one of those it would be time to call 911! So for something as simple, and yet as profound, as breathing in and breathing out we need both to sustain life.

A Paradigm Shift

At this point you might be thinking "Enough, already! I get it!" But the messages that bombard us about staying on that straight and narrow path are just so formidable; we need to reinforce what we know intuitively about navigating change and uncertainty. It is in our DNA to view matters cyclically, but lately nurture appears to have eclipsed nature. It's time to remind ourselves about what is real and natural.

When we scan our true natures, we know, in our heart of hearts, that there are times for building, launching, and stepping out into the world and times when we need to step back and step in to find a new vision for what's next. This phase requires us to make a huge paradigm shift in the way we look at our lives and make choices.

Overlapping the idea of life structure and life transition onto the concept of stepping out and stepping in forms the basic framework for our map on how to navigate change. This process creates four quadrants, each with different guidelines for how to best traverse that phase.

At Centerpoint we have applied a metaphor to this map of a natural cycle with which we are familiar: the seasons of the year. Each phase doesn't occur in each season. Instead, each has qualities and characteristics of a particular season, which makes it more understandable.

We find it helpful to walk through each season, each phase, in a deliberate way. The correlation is direct; the more time spent applying and integrating this approach, the more helpful it becomes as a tool in our daily lives. Chapter 2 offers a high-level visual depiction of the progression of the seasonal phases, while Chapters 4 to 7 present each "season" in detail. Now that we have reviewed the basics, let's look at how to navigate the natural cycles of our lives in a graceful and growth-filled way.

the natural cycles of change™

summer
fruition: make the vision real

- launch
- build
- manage time and energy
- stay on track

fall
completion: reevaluate and let go

- loss of energy
- denial
- feel trapped
- anger
- hold on/hang on
- stress
- bargaining
- prepare for closure
- gratitude

positive plateau

life structure

active, outward, vision, energy

summer fall spring winter

commitment point– "yes"

ending point– "no"

life transition

receptive, inward, no vision, no energy

renewal

spring
creation: reach out/
bridge to creating the dream

- explore options
- creative process
- new knowledge and skills
- find the right fit
- "follow your bliss"
- experimenting and networking

winter
gestation: return to self/
a new vision is born

- relief, fear
- loneliness
- depression
- low self-esteem
- cocooning
- rest, heal
- acceptance
- inspiration

The Natural Cycles of Change:
A Sneak Preview

A FIRST GLANCE AT A MAP, be it of a country or a region, gives us the big picture. Then, with an understanding of the whole, we explore areas of interest or pick a destination and then figure out how to get there, perhaps by the interstate, perhaps by a slower but more interesting route.

If you are someone who likes to start with the big picture, spend a few minutes exploring this visual of the Natural Cycles of Change and the relationship of each season to the whole. As you continue reading you will realize that no direct highway points from winter to summer, nor is there a back road leading from fall to summer. Instead, you will learn how to set your own pace and pick your own routes that progress naturally through the cycles from your current seasons to your new vision, your next destination.

Centerpoint developed this approach and model over time. As our clients have applied it and as the faculty and staff have used it professionally and personally, it has evolved into an extremely useful tool. We invite you to see how you can embrace the natural cycles of change as a lifelong tool for yourself.

> *Seasons is a wise metaphor for the movement of life, I think.*
> *It suggests that life is neither a battlefield nor a game of chance*
> *but something infinitely richer, more promising, more real.*
> *The notion that our lives are like the eternal cycle of the seasons*
> *does not deny the struggle or the joy, the loss or the gain,*
> *the darkness or the light, but encourages us to embrace it all*
> *—and to find in all of it opportunities for growth.*
> —Parker J. Palmer
> from *Let Your Life Speak*

The Space to Find Yourself

Look well into thyself; there is a source of strength
which will always spring up if thou wilt always look there.

—Marcus Aurelius, 121–180 AD

THROUGHOUT MILLENNIA, human beings have heard this Ancient Greek adage: Know thyself. Here is a phrase inscribed in the sixth century BCE at the ancient Temple of Delphi:

I warn you, whoever you are ….
Oh, you who wish to probe the arcanes of nature, if you do not find
within yourself that which you seek, neither shall you be able
to find it outside. If you ignore the excellencies of your own house,
how do you intend to find other excellencies? In you is hidden the treasure
of treasures. Oh, man, know thyself and thou shall know
the Universe and the Gods!

Benjamin Franklin in his 1750 *Poor Richard's Almanack* said, *"There are three things extremely hard: steel, a diamond, and to know one's self."* Knowing oneself is a complex and knotty task—especially because we are constantly changing creatures. In addition, we live in such a faced-paced world, where our to-do lists seem to grow exponentially. How do we create time and space within all the confusion to listen to our truth, our hearts or, as the mystics often called it, the still, small voice within?

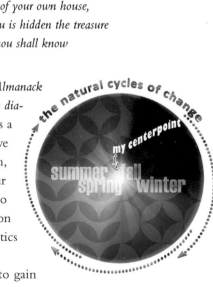

On the cycle, **The Centerpoint** is a place to gain this perspective and find ourselves. As you will soon learn, each time we go through a major transition—and especially through

The only tyrant I accept in this world is the still voice within.

~Mahatma Gandhi

winter, the time between dreams—our ability to listen to ourselves appears to amplify. As we expand our awareness we can more willingly open ourselves to broader possibilities.

To plot the course of our lives and clearly define what we would find meaningful, we need to develop new methods of listening. Instead of searching outside of ourselves, we need to listen to our own hearts, minds, and intuition. It takes different skills to live life from the inside out. We can't underestimate the benefit of simply creating some space, an opening, a centerpoint, to be able to pay attention.

Joseph Campbell said:

This is an absolute necessity for anybody today. You must have a room, or a certain hour or so a day, where you don't know what was in the newspapers this morning, you don't know who your friends are, you don't know what you owe anybody, you don't know what anybody owes you. This is a place where you can simply experience and bring forth what you are and what you might be. This is the place of creative incubation. At first you might find that nothing happens there. But if you have a sacred place and use it, something eventually will happen. Your sacred space is where you can find yourself again and again.

How to Create the Space to Find Yourself

There is no one, right way to do this. We each have our own little and big methods for propping open the doors to our hearts. The first step is to remember what has worked for you in the past.

For example, lying on the couch and listening to a particular piece of music might be an easy way to open up some space; traveling for six weeks in a remote part of the world might be a more self-challenging, all-encompassing experience.

EXERCISE

Use the box that follows to list all your Sources of Renewal, your ways of stepping back and stepping in. Write down things that:

- *help you gain perspective*
- *bring you into the moment*
- *bring back hope*
- *seem to feed something in you*
- *help you sort through something*
- *help you get in touch with yourself*

- *help you "refill the well"*
- *help you take care of yourself*
- *allow you to relax*
- *make you peaceful*
- *are environments that you love*
- *open your heart*

My sources of renewal...

All men's miseries derive from not being able to sit in a quiet room alone.

~Blaise Pascal, French Mathematician, Philosopher and Physicist, 1623–1662

From what you listed, what one, small step can you take today to create some space for renewal for yourself?

The more confusing and overwhelming the transition, the more essential it is to make room for deep listening.

No one can give you better advice than yourself.
—Cicero

Even when we aren't experiencing a major shift in our lives, we still need to stop and, please pardon the worn-out cliché, "smell the roses." When we are busy and engaged in "doing" activities, we still need time for renewal and simply "being."

Pausing the crazy-busy pace of our lives and engaging in activities that help us slow down and renew is just one step. What do we do when we stop?

Listening from My Centerpoint

We often hear the term "active listening" as we learn how to communicate better with others. Developed in 1957 by psychologists Carl Rogers and Richard Farson, such listening is the art of consciously paying attention to what's being said by another to build bridges for understanding and lay the foundation for change. It is also an enormously useful tool when the relationship we're attempting to build is with ourselves.

What I am
is good enough
if I would only
be it openly.
~Carl Rogers

Listening brings about changes in peoples attitudes toward themselves and others; it also brings about changes in their basic values and personal philosophy. People who have been listened to in this new and special way become more emotionally mature, more open to their experiences, less defensive, more democratic, and less authoritarian.
—Rogers and Farson

Genuine listening is hard work. It requires that we are not preoccupied or distracted. We create an intentional space to discern our own voice and feelings. As you create your space to listen notice what grabs your attention as you are listening: Name the feeling that is strongest. Is there a certain place in your body where your feelings are focused? When you stay with that emotion and give it expression, go even deeper and peel away the upper layers to get to the heart of the sensation. If you're sad, concentrate on it longer than you might usually. What are you grieving? If the sadness had a voice, what would it say to you? Ask it questions about what else it needs to verbalize. And then restate this back to yourself so you can make sure you understand it correctly.

Intuition: A Necessary Tool for Listening

Intuition is a holistic and nonlinear method of decision-making. It traces back to the Latin word *intueor* or *intueri*, meaning to contemplate or look within (Zohar and Marshall, 2000). In a linear, climb-the-ladder world, intuition gets short shrift. Often attributed to feminine characteristics, it tends to be belittled and devalued in the "real world."

As the changes occurring all around us continue at warp speed, the benefits of tapping into intuition are gaining interest. In business, those in powerful positions are acknowledging its importance.

> *You cannot ignore your intuition.*
> —Bill Gates

> *My business skills have come from being guided by my intuition.*
> —Oprah Winfrey

> *I've built a multi-billion dollar empire by relying on my gut instinct.*
> —Donald Trump

Antonio was running his own small, successful business. After a few years of expanding, it began to decline, lose money, and generally fail. Antonio was a true entrepreneur and had lots of ideas on how to salvage the business to get it back to its previous level of success. However, nothing he tried worked. He was confused and overwhelmed.

One day, to create some space and renewal for himself, he was sitting quietly, meditating and letting his mind wander. He found himself picturing various slides in his mind's eye. Whatever image appeared, he would examine it and then let it go, replacing it with a new slide. One visualization was a big, old tree in a pot, the roots gnarly and spreading up and out over the rim. In a sudden flash of insight, he grasped that the tree represented himself. He said, "Now I recognize that I've outgrown my container." It became crystal clear to him why his attempts at rebuilding the business were unsuccessful. He was done. Instead of growing it, he took steps to get it into solid enough shape to sell so that he could take time to determine his next steps, which were, at that point, still hazy and vague.

Seek out that particular mental attribute which makes you feel most deeply and vitally alive, along with which comes the inner voice which says, 'This is the real me,' and when you have found that attitude, follow it.

~William James

Sit in reverie,
and watch the
changing color
of the waves
that break
upon the idle
seashore of
the mind.

*~Henry Wadsworth
Longfellow*

Without the space to slow down, stop, and create an opportunity for listening, Antonio would not have been able to figure out what was really happening to him in a timely manner; he could have gone on for quite some time while his business failed and he went further into debt trying to rescue it. We often resist stopping to listen. Instead we feel compelled and are encouraged by others to push through and take action—any action—even though those steps may be counterproductive.

In subsequent chapters we will explore how various parts of our lives revolve around a cyclical model that helps us understand how to navigate change and uncertainty. What about the centerpoint? Do we have to go *'Round and 'round and 'round in the circle game*? Or can we place ourselves at the center of the cycle and live happily ever after?

Living from One's Centerpoint

When we
understand,
we are at the
center of the
circle, and there
we sit while Yes
and No chase
each other
around the
circumference.

~Chuang Tzu

I was fortunate to have a friend who lived until the age of 102. While his body was weakening, his mind was as sharp as a tack. I so enjoyed our conversations because I felt he was living out of his centerpoint. He would talk about starting and losing three businesses in the Depression and his struggles to feed his family during those years. While aware of the drama that persisted in his family, he maintained his perspective—one of kindness and love, never getting caught up in the pettiness. Sitting and talking with him was like basking in rays of sunshine and hope. This is when I realized that maybe, instead of just going 'round and 'round, as we go through the many cycles in life and learn from them, we are perhaps spiraling inward to a place and a life that feels peaceful, centered, and where we can view the full vista without getting mired in life's daily muck.

I just hope I don't have to wait until the age of 102 to get there! The more we create the space to listen and find ourselves, the more we can give of ourselves in a deeper and integral way.

Knowing others is intelligence; knowing yourself is true wisdom.
Mastering others is strength; mastering yourself is true power.
—Tao Te Ching

More Ways to Gain Perspective

The vast majority of us aren't fully enlightened and do get bogged down in our day-to-day lives, so we need to understand how to navigate the normal upheaval and chaos of everyday living. Chapters 4 through 7 decode each phase of the cycles to provide a practical framework for interpreting our experiences and making sense of them from a new perspective.

Inside myself is a place where I live all alone and
that's where you renew your springs that never dry up.
—Pearl S. Buck

None of us will ever accomplish anything excellent or commanding except
when he listens to this whisper which is heard by him alone.
—Ralph Waldo Emerson

Some say that my teaching is nonsense.
Others call it lofty but impractical.
But to those who have looked inside themselves,
this nonsense makes perfect sense. And to those who put it into
practice, this loftiness has roots that go deep.

I have just three things to teach:
simplicity, patience, compassion.
These three are your greatest treasures.
Simple in actions and in thoughts, you return
to the source of being. Patient with both friends and enemies, you
accord with the way things are.
Compassionate toward yourself, you reconcile
all beings in the world.
~Tao Te Ching

The Natural Cycles of Change: Summer

*Summer is the time when one sheds one's tensions with one's clothes,
and the right kind of day is jeweled balm for the battered spirit.
A few of those days and you can become drunk with the belief that
all's right with the world.*
—Ada Louise Huxtable

THE PHASE OF NAVIGATING change with which we tend to be most familiar is Summer; it aligns with the linear, climb the ladder, happily ever after viewpoint that is so prevalent around us. My description of the various stages or "seasons" begins with Summer because it is the one for which we get the most encouragement and support from those around us: our families, friends, work colleagues, and others in our community and society.

Thriving in Summer means that we have a clear vision, goal, dream, or direction and the energy to launch, build, and create it. Remember, we are now in a Life Structure, the upper half of the cycle in which expanding energy allows us to make our mark in the world.

Commitment Point

Summer begins at a Commitment Point. We wholeheartedly say "Yes!" to an external form that our internal vision will take. Anything new requires a lot of time and attention at the start. We need to learn the rules and understand how to navigate this not-yet-traveled route.

For example, think about times when you have embarked on something new—entered a new school, begun a new job, or kindled a new relationship. We

commitment point - yes!

immerse ourselves in these activities and it takes more time and energy at the onset than it will later on.

But, you know what? We don't feel completely drained by how much time is involved; we're energized by it! We are jazzed by the commitment we've made and want to learn all that we can so we will be successful. At the same time we feel a bit overwhelmed by the newness, but it's unlike the overwhelmed feeling we experience when the vision is in decline and our energy is waning.

Looking at us from the outside in, our friends and family might think that our lives are way out of balance. They may say *"We never see you anymore. You're always at school, work, or with that new person!"* To us, though, our lives don't feel unbalanced; they feel just perfect! It's delightful to immerse in this newfound connection and spend as much time as possible in it.

If we've just begun a new job, it's thrilling to feel absorbed in the business, to learn as much as we can, and to bring our vision to fruition. Oh, yes, it can be a bit scary too, but that doesn't preclude our enthusiasm for this new experience. We feel good about the commitment we've made and we're determined to see it through. In career terms, we call this the Career Management phase because we're moving in a direction that feels vital and satisfying. Now the goals are to stay on track, advance, fine-tune our balance, and hone our leadership skills.

Even in common situations, like embarking on a vacation or attending a conference, we experience that initial phase of disorientation, followed by figuring out how everything works. How do I get from my hotel to the restaurant or to that session room? After a short while, it becomes easier and even second nature.

Summer allows us the opportunity to advance from challenge to mastery in whatever part of our lives we are building. As we spend more time immersed and learning, we gain confidence and grow in our ability to manage the challenges that inevitably follow. We also identify more solidly with whatever we are creating; this becomes a building block in how we think about and distinguish ourselves from others. If someone at a party asks "What do you do?" We are proud to say that "I'm a teacher" or "I'm a parent" or "I'm a college student."

One of the important "gifts" that we receive in Summer is increased competency in the area of life on which we are focusing. Throughout this season we can also:

- Affirm and strengthen our identity via our accomplishments.
- Gain recognition from others because of those achievements.
- Find ways to be of service to others.
- Reap financial rewards.
- Feel more connected to the external world.
- Develop a sense of mastery in our area of Summer focus.
- Make our mark in some way.

Challenges in Summer

Summer may sound ideal—the "straight and narrow" often equated with success—but it also has its challenges.

- **Committing to a Vision** Selecting one specific direction in which to head can be difficult for some; creative and artistic people frequently find this to be the case. While choosing one vision to pursue feels cozy and secure to some, others see it as overly constraining. For the latter, opting for one path over another means eliminating possibilities and letting go of viable and exciting opportunities. That's scary and may deter some people from fully committing to any vision.
- **Staying on Track** Launching a vision is a very different skill from growing it and succeeding at it. It is especially difficult if what we have set out to accomplish is something large that will take time to manifest. What skills must we develop and what people must we gather to continue to build our vision?
- **Economizing Focus, Time, and Energy** A lot of energy surrounds any vision we create; that energy can also inadvertently generate distractions along the way. Others hear our enthusiasm and get excited by our passion, and favorable opportunities can seemingly arise out of nowhere. By our prudent choices of how we spend our time and energy, we can more easily accomplish what we have set out to do and avoid being sidetracked.

A late summer
garden has a
tranquility
found no
other time
of the year.

~William Longgood

- **Maintaining Connection with the Vision** If we neglect to continuously revisit the heart of our vision, we can lose sight of our true goal. It's sometimes easy to overlook the importance of regularly connecting with the vision because of the many competing activities in our lives. Remember, the energy at this stage of the change cycle is contagious and the "noise" level in our lives can be high. The more we can consistently remember what we want, the easier it is to make decisions that help us attain it.

- **Cultivating Patience and Persistence** Growing a vision in Summer takes a lot of hard work. We can get burned out by how much of ourselves we need to pour into making the vision real. We can also forget to take time for renewal, to build in vacations, and find some semblance of balance in our lives. What reminders do we need that a vision may take a while to transpire and that we need to engage in self-care all along the way?

Positive Plateau

As we move through Summer and progress from challenge to mastery, the amount of energy the vision takes evens out a bit. Things are easier: at work we have learned how to delegate more and feel more confident and competent. Our most important relationships feel solid; we feel we can count on them. We have reached what we call a Positive Plateau.

positive plateau

At times the word "plateau" is used in a negative sense: hitting the glass ceiling, being stagnant. Instead, think of it as positive, a time or place when or where we have achieved a great deal of what we set out to accomplish. It's a place where we are living our vision and are feeling enthused by it. In a way, the Positive Plateau is a resting place, a mini-cycle in itself, where we can reap the benefits of all that we have built. It's like a summer garden in full bloom where we are able to harvest and enjoy the fruits of our labors.

At this point many people talk about balance. They often say "I want all that I've built and the rest of my life as well."

The most important things to ask ourselves at the Positive Plateau are:

- "Is my vision still alive?"
- "Do I still love [fill in the blank]?"
- "What's my energy level like? Do I still have lots of enthusiasm to continue to build my vision?"

If you've read my bio, you will see that my career vision has been alive for more than 30 years. That's an awfully long time, but I was lucky to be able to find my life's work early in my adulthood. For anyone who's ever met me and talked with me about life and career renewal, you can immediately tell that I've still got tons of energy for this field. Truthfully, though, if I had to do the same thing day after day, year after year in my job, I'd be bored out of my mind!

As I cycle through my own Positive Plateaus, I encounter many smaller stepping-backs to figure out how to do what I do better, to try new ideas and strategies, to continue to learn and grow, and to find ways to contribute more. My vision is still very much alive; I continue to evolve it, and I am able to assist in far-reaching ways. (This book is a case in point!)

However, different personalities have different challenges. While, like all of us, I have lots of struggles in the other parts of my life, Positive Plateauing in my career isn't one of them. For others, again especially those who are extremely creative or artistic, plateauing may be one of the most difficult things with which to contend. These folks love the initial, start-up stages of a vision but when it reaches the Positive Plateau, they get tired of it. They say "been there, done that, now what's next?" and they're off and running in an entirely new direction. Do that a few times and, for some, exhaustion may set in if there is no resting place, no reaping the benefits of what they built.

Many industries also experience this type of challenge. Take the information technology field, for instance. Look at how far and how fast technology has developed over the past 25 years. IT professionals are truly on the cutting edge and must keep one step ahead of their competitors—absolutely no resting allowed. That may be one reason why so many people get burned out and why these jobs have

Rest is not idleness, and to lie sometimes on the grass on a summer day listening to the murmur of water, or watching the clouds float across the sky, is hardly a waste of time.

~John Lubbock

a great deal of turnover; it's very difficult to keep up that kind of pace over the long haul.

That may also be the reason why many companies fail. They don't take the time to step back to find a new vision for what they need to develop next. They feel like they have to remain continually in motion or they'll fall behind. It's ironic, though, because the stepping back will get them where they need to go, if they could only see the benefit of doing the internal work.

Different parts of our lives can be in different seasons. As I mentioned earlier, my own career is in a Positive Plateau and has been for a long while now. However, if I look at other areas of my life, in one particular aspect I have a difficult time plateauing. That's my sense of self, my core. I describe this part of me as the one that periodically goes back into therapy to learn more about myself. This part values growth beyond anything else. Once I examine something in myself that may be keeping me stuck or dissatisfied and then find ways to heal it, I want to move right on to the next part of myself that needs attention. There's no stopping to "smell the flowers" and fully appreciate what I just learned and healed. I'm ready to jump right into what's calling me to grow next and step up to work on that.

A Positive Plateau gives us an opportunity to see that it is not just "okay" to appreciate what we have accomplished, but it is valuable to acknowledge how proud we are of ourselves. We ought to feel good about all the hard work we put into making that vision happen. In thinking about this experience as a garden, we realize we can harvest all the bounty of what we planted and then take time to savor an extraordinary meal made from that abundance.

> What is one to say about June, the time of perfect young summer, the fulfillment of the promise of the earlier months, and with as yet no sign to remind one that its fresh young beauty will ever fade.
>
> ~Gertrude Jekyll

Mini-Transitions

Summer typically isn't one smooth journey or trajectory. Smaller changes often occur along the way. We call these **Mini-Transitions.**

In Mini-Transitions we are not finding an entirely new vision, we are simply uncovering a new structure that will fit us better. It's creating a new container for a vision that is still alive.

My Personal Mini-Transitions

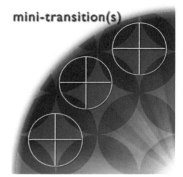

mini-transition(s)

As an example, let me share with you a bit more about my career path. In 1981 I became a career counseling professional in a New York City university setting, working with undergraduate and graduate students entering a variety of fields. While the choice sounded interesting and a good fit, I remember making the decision to commit to it for a variety of reasons: I wanted to apply what I was learning in my own graduate classes at the time and theory alone without simultaneously seeing its practical application has never held a great deal of excitement for me. Another advantage of the job was the tuition reimbursement benefit so that I wouldn't have to go further into debt. And, while the job didn't pay much, a very inexpensive Manhattan apartment fell in my lap the same week I was offered the position. I was convinced this was the right next step for me.

In addition to these logical reasons for accepting the job, I also had an intuitive sense that it would be a good fit. I was right; I immediately found myself loving the work. My career Summer was humming along until my second year. I then began feeling less satisfied and wasn't sure why. I had to step back and ask some important questions. Was it the career itself? The kinds of students I was working with? My colleagues? I was unsure about what wasn't working for me.

After taking some time for introspection, I realized that it was the environment. I loved my colleagues and higher education in general, but I found that this particular university setting was missing some essential pieces. A better fit for me was a place where I could feel a true part of the larger academic community and enjoy more autonomy and flexibility. As I began to focus on other opportunities I happened to meet someone who told me about an opening at the law school where he worked. (We will talk more about the roles that luck, synchronicity, and clarity play when we get to the Spring chapter.) To my surprise, even though I had never assisted lawyers and knew nothing about the legal profession, they hired me anyway. I loved the spirit of the place and knew this was just the community I was looking for.

After several years there I was still in love with my work and the

> Love is to the heart what the summer is to the farmer's year it brings to harvest all the loveliest flowers of the soul.
>
> ~*Author unknown*

law school, but was feeling increasingly unhappy with relationships. Why was I meeting all the wrong men? I needed some help to sort through my questions. Through therapy I realized that the real issue wasn't about my relationships with others, it was about my relationship with myself. As I developed a better sense of who I was and what I needed, I was able to deepen my self-confidence and self-esteem. From that understanding came a surprising realization that I was living in the wrong geographical area!

While it took me a few years to figure out my vision for where I truly belonged and to uncover it, I did find the perfect place for me (Seattle). But what was I going to do work-wise? My vision for career counseling was still very much alive, but I couldn't move my job to the West Coast. After a smaller stepping back to determine what aspects of my career I wanted to keep and what I wanted to shift a bit, I began exploring opportunities. This was another Mini-Transition: changing the "container" but not changing the entire vision.

> Ah, summer, what power you have to make us suffer and like it.
>
> ~Russell Baker

Re-Structuring vs. Re-Visioning

You may have noticed a common thread throughout these examples of my career Mini-Transitions. I chose each of them. I made the decision to change my work and living environments. It does not always occur this way. Sometimes outside forces make the choices for us. For example, when we get laid off from a job, here's the first question we need to ask ourselves: "Is my vision still alive?" Usually because we are in shock, it is the last thing we *think* to ask ourselves. We need to determine if the direction in which we have been heading is still exciting to us. If it is, then we need to step back some to give ourselves time to grieve the job loss and then revisit our goals to see what, if any, course corrections we'd like to make at this point.

Helpful Summer Activities

Here are a few activities that you may find helpful in Summer:

MAINTAIN MOMENTUM
- **Stay True to the Vision** Keep the vision close at hand and revisit it regularly. Refer to it whenever any course corrections are needed or opportunities arise.

- **Mini-Renewals** Summer requires a great deal of effort and energy. Remember, we need to take time for "refilling our well" along the way. And don't forget to take vacations!
- **Emotional Support** Nowhere along the cycle do you have to journey alone. Ask for help from people who will encourage you and your vision.

BUILD SKILLS

- **Self-Management Skills** The more we know about ourselves, the stronger we are. The stronger we are, the more we can contribute to others and make a bigger difference.
- **Time Management Skills** When we are excited about something, there will never be enough hours in the day to engage in all we want to do. We need to prioritize and make choices about what we have the most energy for and what will effectively advance the vision.
- **People Management Skills** Building something that requires solid, professional relationships for success, also requires positive people management skills. Remember the adage: You can attract more flies with honey than with vinegar.
- **Communication Skills** A vital tool in communicating is being able to listen effectively. Most of us are never taught how to do that. It's worth learning.
- **Relationship Building Skills** No matter what the vision, we live in a world of relationships. How do we continue to develop connection and community through every step along the way?

Of all the wonders of nature, a tree in summer is perhaps the most remarkable; with the possible exception of a moose singing "Embraceable You" in spats.

~Woody Allen

KEEP ON TRACK

- **Goal Setting, Planning** We need some level of organization to accomplish our vision and goals. If we don't naturally come by this talent, we need to find others who can help us cultivate it or do it for us.
- **Problem Solving** Obstacles will inevitably arise along the way. Taking the time to compose creative questions can help us find innovative solutions. Be careful not to jump to something new or shove our way through too quickly. That may alleviate our immediate discomfort of the stuck feelings but not address the underlying problems.

- **Economy of Effort** This means continually choosing activities that allow us to get the most benefit from the least amount of effort.

ENGAGE CREATIVITY

- **Brainstorm Alternatives** Sometimes the best ideas come from the collaboration of many brains. Gather people together who "think outside the box" for a creative session to handle any obstacles you may encounter in your path towards your vision.
- **Think Outside the Box Yourself** Use an intuitive, right-brain, out-there approach when addressing any problem to be solved. Often the best solutions arise from the most off-the-wall inspirations.

Summer Is Only One Phase

In summer, the song sings itself.

~William Carlos Williams

Much of the information on the nature of Summer and how to best navigate it probably is not new to any of us. It is what we are told we need to do to be successful in the world. Summer is the straight and narrow, climbing the ladder portion of the cycle. But as you can see, it's not the only piece of the puzzle. There are three more quadrants to navigate.

And They Lived Happily Ever After...

Stephen Sondheim wrote the music and lyrics for the 1987 Broadway show *Into the Woods*, based on a book by James Lapine. The first half of the show intertwines vignettes of familiar fairy tales with which we grew up. We heard these stories over and over throughout our childhoods and have passed them along to our children and our children's children. They are ingrained in us. At the conclusion of the stories we hear the familiar phrase "And they lived happily ever after."

But wait, the stories don't really end there! After intermission, *Into The Woods* goes on to relate what happens AFTER happily ever after. Things get complicated: Cinderella's and Rapunzel's princes go off into the woods where they meet and become enamored of Snow White and Sleeping Beauty. Questions arise such as, *What do we do with a dead giant in the backyard?* Many lessons are learned. This is real life—the messy, confusing parts that no one tells us about nor explains how to handle.

Maybe it's time to redraw our picture of what life looks like and reframe the idea of happiness. Now there is a way to navigate what is after "happily ever after." What follows is an approach that helps us learn from the losses and difficult times so we can renew ourselves and live lives that are more meaningful and growth filled.

> *When summer gathers up her robes of glory,*
> *And, like a dream, glides away.*
> —Sarah Helen Whitman

The Natural Cycles of Change: Fall

Change is a measure of time and, in the autumn, time seems speeded up.
What was is not and never again will be; what is is change.
—Edwin Way Teale

EVER HEAR OF A MILESTONE movie in the 1960s called *"The End-less Summer?"* Once winter hit California, several surfers traveled the world's summer shores to find and film the perfect wave. The movie's plot exemplifies the myth that Summer is the best place to be and is the only worthwhile undertaking. *Fascinating side comment:* In the film they discovered that, in Australia and New Zealand, the surfing was exceptional in the winter season.

We are constantly bombarded with messages from all ranks about the intrinsic worth of Summer. Why would we even consider being anywhere else? Because we must. No matter how much we wish it weren't so, everything is in a constant state of change. For life to exist, chaos must be present. So what happens in our lives when things shift and begin to decline? It catapults us into the…

In Summer we felt a part of things and were immersed in the vision. In Fall it feels like we are on the outside looking in. We reevaluate, asking questions like:

- Is there more to life than this?
- Am I just getting old?
- Am I expecting too much of life?

Decreased Energy, No Vision

decline ↗ ↗ ↗ ↗

Our energy has shifted. It feels like that old spark is gone and it takes effort just to get ourselves out of bed each day. Our vision, our dream, has died. One of three things has occurred:

- We've outgrown that vision. What seemed like such a good fit at one point now feels too small for us. What was once big enough is now limiting us. We need something more.
- We realize that the vision we set out to achieve is not what we expected. This experience is described perfectly by Joseph Campbell in his statement, *"Sometimes, you get to the top of a ladder and discover you're at the wrong building."*
- Or, we're on track but our vision is taken away from us by circumstances, like a layoff, an accident, or death, or something as ordinary as an argument with our partner. Losing something often makes us question the entire vision and ask ourselves, "Is this what I really want anyway?"

Denial

denial

Our first reaction to such shifting is denial. We say to ourselves, "Oh, things aren't *that* bad." Denial is our way of avoiding what's really going on. We try to distance or numb ourselves. The result is that we are unable to take any steps. This avoidance can show up as "vegging out": sitting in front of the TV and channel surfing, obsessively playing computer games, or perhaps keeping incessantly busy so that we don't even allow ourselves a moment to think about what's changing.

Sometimes the avoidance shows up in more serious and self-destructive ways. Those who have had a history of alcohol or substance abuse, for instance, may find themselves reverting, even unconsciously, to those behaviors to numb themselves to the reality of the situation.

In terms of our jobs, the denial usually appears in two ways:

- We work harder to prove to ourselves that nothing has changed. However, since our energy has waned, even when exerting extra effort we achieve fewer results.
- We tell ourselves we just need a vacation. We had a client who was experiencing several major transitions in his life. He had registered for an all-day workshop focused on the Centerpoint Natural Cycles of Change so he could understand more about how to deal with those changes. The week before the workshop he called to cancel. He said that he had just returned from a vacation and was feeling so much better; the workshop was now unnecessary. One of our career counselors, who had previously talked with him and had perceived that he was in a major shift that wouldn't be solved with a vacation, asked him to call back in three days to check in again. He called. And he came to the workshop. His renewal didn't last very long. Almost immediately he was back to feeling burned-out and questioning his direction in his life and work.

Sometimes it is quite difficult to face the situation we are experiencing. An inner conflict is unfolding during this stage of Fall. Our hearts are saying "This isn't working anymore and I need something more." At the same time our heads kick in and say "Wait a minute, don't do anything rash!" One of our clients sent us a note that described this stage really well. It said, *"I don't even want to write about these changes that are happening in my life. I'm afraid I might do something... and I'm afraid I might not."*

Anger

Because of this conflict, we find that stress has taken hold and is beginning to build. The next stage of Fall is anger. Denial, anger...as you can see, we are overlapping Elisabeth Kübler-Ross's stages of grief on the cycle. Whether major or mini, every change we experience is a loss of what came before.

What previously energized us now entraps us. We feel

victimized, without choice, and as though things are entirely out of our control. Our anger at this stage will be directed inwardly or expressed outwardly.

The inwardly directed anger shows up as self-criticism. We feel dreadful about not being able to accomplish what we could when we were in Summer. We ask ourselves questions like "What's wrong with me?" and "Why can't things be like they were?" We are so adept at beating ourselves up! But no matter how often people tell us to be kind to ourselves, we simply can't: we want things as they were, even if we were miserable with them that way. The old adage "the devil you know is better than the devil you don't" comes to mind. At least that way we can be certain about something—our despondency.

Anger turned inward can lead to stress, depression, lack of appropriate assertive behavior, and mood swings. Consequently, these can lead to physical symptoms and, if we are not consciously aware of what's happening, can transform into debilitating illnesses—a downward, destructive spiral.

Externally expressed anger is focused on everyone and everything else *except* ourselves. This is the stage where we complain, rant, rave, blame, and then complain even more vehemently. We complain so much that friends telephone us less frequently. Or, they stop calling altogether. It's extremely difficult to listen to someone who appears to be taking no responsibility for the current situation and who is blaming everyone else. This behavior pattern ambushes many of us when we feel trapped and out of control.

While this stage is difficult for us and for those around us, realizing that we are angry is a good sign. It means we are not in denial and that we are taking steps to move through the change process.

A *caveat*: Kübler-Ross acknowledges that the stages of grief don't necessarily happen in sequence and that we cycle through the stages in various orders and for varying amounts of time. By using her framework and the other concepts that make up the Natural Cycles of Change, they help us to make sense of our experiences. Don't try to crowbar yourself into just one spot on the cycle; use this model as a tool so you can better navigate the changes and uncertainty in your life and career.

> October's poplars are flaming torches lighting the way to winter.
> ~Nova Bair

Bargaining

Bargaining reveals itself in the form of a rescue fantasy. It often sounds like *"If only…"*: if only my boss was different, if only my kids were different, if only my relationship was different, then everything would be okay. We hope that someone or something will rush in to make it all better, even going so far as to sweep us off our feet. This white knight in shining armor can take various forms. We may have heard ourselves or someone else wish the most common rescue fantasy of all: *"If I just won the lottery!"* Another rescue fantasy is logging onto Monster.com and expecting that the perfect position will just pop up on the screen. Then we can simply wave bye-bye to whatever has been trapping us and move on to our next choice without any more angst or discomfort.

The Quick Fix

At times, something—a new job, relationship, idea—will turn up that appears to be our next logical step. It looks reasonable and feels familiar. We tell ourselves that this next [fill in the blank] is just what we need to go riding off into the sunset and live happily ever after. There's just one major problem. Remember that in Fall we have no clear vision and not much energy. That "sunset" we are going toward is not grounded in anything. Why are we so anxious to pick something new? At least it gets us out of what doesn't fit any longer. The problem is that this choice isn't advancing us toward something; we are just

Jumping from Fall to Summer with no clear vision and a lack of energy

escaping something else. We call this strategy the Quick Fix. With no vision and a lack of energy undergirding this choice, it cannot last. After some possible engaging and creative beginnings, inevitably and without a doubt we will find ourselves back in Fall.

A "rebound romance" is an example of a Quick Fix that doesn't work. You know the progression: we've broken off with one person and then immediately get involved with someone new, which again, doesn't work out. The quick fix in this instance can be described as: same relationship, different face. We have no stirring vision for what we want in the next person, so that connection becomes a re-creation of the relationship that just ended.

Interestingly and at certain times, though, a Quick Fix can be an excellent strategy. It helps test some possibilities when unsure if we are still enthusiastic about our vision. If I just change some of my responsibilities, will I enjoy this more? If I change departments, or bosses, will my vision be back on track? If I can train myself to squeeze the toothpaste tube from the bottom, will my partner be happier with me? By experimenting, we can give ourselves more information from which to make a decision. But we must be careful to make these choices consciously and identify what we are learning about ourselves. If we don't, we may feel like we are simply jumping from one thing to the next and not making much progress. If we were to draw a visual, it might look like this:

Tried that...

...didn't work

A career example is the story of "Tim," a successful government lawyer. Over the course of his life he had many academic and athletic achievements. Things seemed to come easily to him and he was consistently recognized for his successes. He did well in college and law school and chose to enter public service. However, he felt that, by working in government, he was less competent than his colleagues who were employed in law firms. He thought that he needed to give the law firm setting a chance and prove to himself and others that he could "make it there."

Tim left public service and joined a firm, but it didn't work out and he was asked to leave his position. Instead of seeing this choice of setting as simply a bad fit for him, he was devastated because he believed he had failed for the first time in his life. Being on unemployment was further evidence that something was wrong with him. He took the first job that came along, with another law firm similar to the previous one. Tim was determined to make this job work, no matter what—a typical Quick Fix.

Three months later, he lost that job too. That firm was having financial difficulties and he was laid off. Even more adamant that he wasn't going to fail, he found a similar position at yet *another* law firm. Going from one law firm to another was another form of rebounding. Three months later he was let go from that job This time, though, that wasn't the only thing that ended. A week later his wife told him she was leaving him. The people from whom he was renting his house let him know that they were moving back into town and he needed to be out in a month.

Tim was devastated. He called Centerpoint and told me he was thinking about moving back to the Midwest where he grew up. But there wasn't anything in the Midwest that Tim was moving toward; instead he was running away from what he felt he was lacking.

During our conversation we discussed how important it was for him to step back and consider what this all meant to him and to uncover his vision. Fortunately, one of Centerpoint's four-day retreats was coming up and Tim decided he needed some help in asking these important questions of himself. He registered for the retreat.

By this time you would think nothing else could go wrong in his life, right? Well, on his way to the retreat, his car exploded. He wasn't physically hurt or endangered, but the car was unsalvageable. We sent someone to pick him up and drive him to the retreat. When we are experiencing so much loss, it's sometimes difficult to ask for help. We were glad that we could support him throughout this time.

At the outset of the retreat, Tim was quite resistant. The process of how he "ought to" figure out what was next for him—just think about it, quickly map it all out, make a decision, and take action—wasn't working. His analytical, problem-solving side was getting in the way of really listening to what his heart needed. He didn't feel comfortable completely letting go of his old ways of making things happen, despite the evidence that they weren't working now.

Eventually, Tim was able to let go and find a way to tap into his

Swinging
on delicate
hinges the
Autumn Leaf
Almost off the
stem

~Jack Kerouac

passion and vision at the retreat. Look for more of his story when we cover Winter in the next chapter.

At this point in Fall, letting go is exactly what's needed. We have to get to an ending point where we can say "No" and realize that the structure we've been trying to make work is no longer viable.

What Kind of Risk Taker Are You?

Our comfort with quick fixes can correspond to our risk-taking styles. Some find it easy to leap into something new and others have an ability to stay with something as long as needed to make it work, no matter the odds. Both styles are beneficial and, at times, both can get us stuck.

Those who thrive in the new and adventurous seem to be able to leave something quickly and without a lot of angst. A case in  point is a client whose career involved an extraordinary level of comfort for risk taking—jumping out of airplanes. When Bill was bored with his work, he would pick an entirely new direction, move to another part of the country, and change his primary relationship—simultaneously. For example, as he tired of his career as a goldsmith in New Mexico, he picked something out of the blue that he thought sounded fun; he moved to Florida to work at SeaWorld. No longer finding that job interesting, he ran across an opportunity to plan large banquets in Colorado. It appealed to him and fit his needs—for a while, anyway. After repeating this pattern several times and still not feeling satisfied with his choices, he determined that his *modus operandi* wasn't working and that he wanted to select his next career with more care and thought. The greatest challenge for Bill was to slow down enough so he could step back to find a vision that was grounded. To *not* jump immediately to something new was one of the most difficult experiences of his life.

Those who are able to make things work against all odds have an opposite challenge. I have to admit that I fall into this category myself.

People with this style are highly capable at accomplishing things, even those that appear seemingly impossible. So how do we know when it's finally time to let go and move on? I'm reminded of a quote by the speaker and author Alan Cohen, who said, "When I let go of something, I leave claw marks!" The overriding challenge, then, is to know when to cease acting. Instead, we have to find a way to release our hold, and walk away from, an unachievable dream. This decision provokes feelings of failure, disappointment, and regret.

Heading Toward No

The thorny part is that we have to let go, say goodbye, and close out a chapter *without* knowing our next big step. At the least, that's daunting; at the most, it's terrifying. At Centerpoint we share a reading by Danaan Parry called *The Parable of the Trapeze: Turning the Fear of Transformation into the Transformation of Fear.* It describes the gist of this stage using an apt metaphor—trapeze bars. Here's the section that describes this phase of Fall:

Sometimes I feel that my life is a series of trapeze swings.
I'm either hanging on to a trapeze bar swinging along or, for a few moments
in my life, I'm hurtling across space in between trapeze bars.
Most of the time, I spend my life hanging on for dear life
to my trapeze-bar-of-the-moment. It carries me along at a certain steady rate
of swing and I have the feeling that I'm in control of my life.
I know most of the right questions and even some of the answers.
But every once in a while as I'm merrily (or even not-so-merrily)
swinging along, I look out ahead of me into the distance and what do I see?
I see another trapeze bar swinging toward me. It's empty and I know,
in that place in me that knows, that this new trapeze bar
has my name on it. It is my next step, my growth, my aliveness coming
to get me. In my heart of hearts I know that, for me to grow, I must release
my grip on this present, well-known bar and move to the new one.
Each time it happens to me I hope (no, I pray) that I won't have
to let go of my old bar completely before I grab the new one.
But in my knowing place, I know that I must totally release my grasp
on my old bar and, for some moment in time, I must hurtle across space
before I can grab onto the new bar....

What enables us to let go of that old trapeze bar and say "no" at the ending point? On our way to "no" we encounter what we refer to as trigger events or wake-up calls.

Trigger Events/Wake-up Calls

These can be external or internal. External wake-up calls are occurrences that makes us sit up and smell the coffee. If we have been experiencing stress throughout Fall, it could be our own health that takes the toll. It's not uncommon for our body's support areas to buckle under the pressure: neck, back, knees, feet. Or we might suffer ailments like chronic fatigue syndrome or even carpal tunnel if we rely on the computer for our livelihood. We are always amazed at Centerpoint to find a disproportionately large number of clients with broken legs. Talk about stopping you in your tracks!

At times, it's someone else's health that is the trigger. A person our own age (or younger) has a sudden and unexpected heart attack or dies, prompting us to rethink what we want. "Julie" was a young woman in her thirties who attended one of Centerpoint's retreats. Julie's trigger event was the death of her best friend, who was her same age. Her friend died in a fall off a cliff in Alaska where she was tagging falcons. Julie realized that her friend was out there, doing what she truly loved, while Julie was sitting behind her desk, dying. At that point Julie knew she had to do something different.

My husband's wake-up call was getting laid off. He knew for several years that he was done with the position he was in but couldn't find the motivation to step back and figure out what was right for him. When he heard he was losing his job, he said he felt remorse for about two seconds. Then the relief kicked in and, not having to put up with his discontent and frustration any longer, he was absolutely thrilled.

Trigger events can also be internal. In our heart of hearts, we just know that we have to end something. It's like "the straw that breaks the camel's back." We get to "no," this isn't working any longer, and we have to let go. We reach an ending point.

Ending Point

An ending can be the leaving of something, e.g., a project, job, relationship, or way of doing something. Or it can be an internal acknowledgment and decision to let go. It's when we tell ourselves something like "I'm out of here in six months."

ending point - no!

Arriving at an ending point in a relationship doesn't always mean that we have to let go of that special someone. It could mean admitting that the connection no longer has a sustainable vision and no longer works. We have to let go of it and step back to uncover whether there is enough of a bond to develop an entirely new vision. Many people, however, find that process difficult and sometimes will completely end the relationship without stopping to pose the hard questions. Perhaps this is one reason divorce is so common.

For most of us, endings are not easy. One word aptly describes the emotion we feel immediately before we are ready to say no and let go—terror! This is why people use graphic images of cliffs to describe what they are going through.

One gentleman who came to Centerpoint told us that he knew he was done with the career he had been in but had no idea what was coming up next. He said it felt as though there was a cliff on one side of him and he was hanging on by his fingernails because he knew that was over. And there was a cliff on the other side and he was hanging on by his fingernails there too because he had no clue about where he was headed. He then looked down and saw a bottomless pit below him. He found himself slowly sinking down into it because he didn't have a firm grasp on either side.

Another image that we often use to illustrate this stage is from the movie *Indiana Jones and the Last Crusade*. Indy's father—played by the great Sean Connery—had been shot and lay dying on the temple floor. The only way Indy could save his father's life was to retrieve the water from the Holy Grail. In true Indiana Jones form, he had to go through several tests for which he was given specific clues. If he was successful, he could then get the Grail and rescue his father.

He successfully made it through several challenges—of course by the skin of his teeth—and arrived at an aperture in a mountain. In front of him, about 30 feet away, he could see the door to the room of the Grail. He encountered a sizeable problem, however; a vast, deep chasm lay between him and the door. A pebble near his foot tumbled into it and he didn't even hear it hit bottom. Scary! The clue Indiana Jones had been given was "a leap from the lion's mouth" or "a leap of faith."

He knows he can't go back; returning to his dying father is not an option. He must move forward. So placing his hand on his heart, closing his eyes, he takes a step out while fully expecting to fall into the abyss. Instead, he's astounded. His foot lands on an invisible bridge that couldn't be seen by the eye. He makes it across to the room and after a few more tests he retrieves the Grail to save his father's life.

Interestingly, a workshop attendee of ours pointed out that, with Indiana Jones's first step onto the bridge, the entire bridge didn't just suddenly appear. He could only see what was right in front of his toes so, in effect, with each step he had to reinforce his personal conviction to move ahead.

The lesson here is when the fog is so thick you can't see where you are going, it is sometimes wise to stop trying. Just focus on your feet and your next, immediate, small stride. You may be able to get reoriented by either standing still for a bit or by taking tiny, baby steps.

*I love the leaves
I do not know why.
Is it their colors
or how they fly?
They crunch
and crinkle
Under my feet;
I pile them up
And take a leap!*

~Beth Paulsen

Mini-Transition(s) in Fall

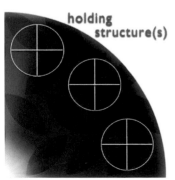

holding structure(s)

As in Summer, we can also experience smaller, temporary cycles in Fall. We call them **Holding Structures.** We realize that the vision has died; it is over. In preparing for whatever is ending, we need time to put things in order.

As squirrels in fall gather as many acorns as they can for the uncertain intensity of winter, we need to put our affairs in order to plan for our own time between dreams. Financial planning helps because we often think we can't do what we really want to because we believe we just can't afford it. We need to question this assumption. The first step is to draft a budget of how we are spending our money. By avoiding this essential step, we often eliminate many of our future possibilities. Once we know where our money is going, we can then ask questions and make choices about what we are willing to change to get what we really want.

Sometimes, to have time to ask even these questions, we need to renegotiate the parameters of our current work, e.g., hours, responsibilities, who we report to, those we manage. Many of us are in jobs that consume great amounts of time during the week. If we are in Summer, we are energized by what we can accomplish. In Fall, it just drains us.

A former client, "Paula," was working for one of those big companies where you get paid for 40 hours a week but you are expected to work 80. She was burned out, but to even think about leaving the job was terrifying for her. She decided to negotiate a three-fourths position at 30 hours per week with the same employer. As you can imagine, that job started to expand beyond those time constraints. She needed to learn some healthy boundary-setting skills.

Whenever the job threatened to spill over into more hours, she would go into her boss and ask "Would you prefer me to work on this project or that one since I don't have time for both?" Freeing up some hours gave her an opening to begin career counseling. This is a great example of a Holding Structure because Paula was able to remain at her company while she was planning a longer-term and deeper transition.

Another client, "Anne," was a CFO in a smaller company. She was going to be laid off and was thrilled about it. She was absolutely done with being a financial professional and emotionally had felt this way for at least the past six months. Even before her job ended, she enrolled in the Passion Search Workshop at Centerpoint so she could clarify her vision for what would be next.

As her vision started to gain focus for the future, she decided she wanted to build in a two-year sabbatical so that she could sail around the world before she stepped into an entirely new direction. Anne was in the midst of planning for the trip and preparing financially to make this dream happen. At the same time she got a call from another company that was looking for a CFO. She had heard such positive things about this particular business that she decided to go for an interview. Then she panicked—she knew she didn't want to be a CFO any longer, what was she thinking? Instead, she set up an hour-long career counseling appointment.

When Anne came in she was concerned that she was jumping into a Quick Fix. Was she trying to be back in Summer with this career that she was positive she wanted to leave? She was afraid she'd get trapped in the field forever and be unable to live her true dream. Should she cancel the interview with this new company?

When asked why she was considering the job, her response was immediate, "It'll get me the sailboat more quickly!" Her vision was still on target; she wouldn't be taking this job to remain in the financial field but to be able to make her two-year sabbatical come true. Then we discussed what it would take to approach this opportunity as a Holding Structure.

She sought several things from this job. One, she wanted to work with the company's affiliates in South America so she could brush up her Spanish for the sailing trip. Two, she wanted to be able to telecommute one to two days per week. And three, she needed to delay starting the job for a month and half because she needed more renewal time. The most important part for her was that she was willing to walk away at any time because, while she could do the job well and could contribute much to the company, she knew it wasn't her life's work.

Anne interviewed and got the offer for the job. As she negotiated her requirements, they said yes to the South American affiliates, yes to the telecommuting, but they needed her to start work the next day. She told them that they would be happier with her if she could take the time off because she'd have more to give to the position and the company. They countered with more money. Even with the enticement of a higher salary, Anne was willing to abandon the opportunity if she didn't get everything she defined as important to her in this Holding Structure. She turned them down. They relented. They hired her and gave her the month and a half off and she was able to speed up her plan to be on the high seas.

Holding Structures are very different from what we might call holding patterns. Holding Structures are conscious choices we make to give ourselves the time we need to close out a chapter. Holding patterns are unconscious and find us doing the same old thing over and over because we're used to and comfortable with it. (Remember: "the devil we know…?")

We often find holding patterns in relationships. We're not willing to open up the question of what's not working because it threatens way too many things. "We are staying together for the children" is a common excuse but, really, how healthy and loving an environment is it for the children if their parents don't relate on an intimate and deep level?

We sometimes refer to people in holding patterns as "sleepwalkers" in life. Something has to die in them so they can keep going. If they were really alive and fully aware of their misery, it would probably kill them. Are there areas of your life in which you are currently sleepwalking?

> We must let go of the life we have planned, so as to have the life that is waiting for us. The old skin has to be shed before the new one can come.
>
> ~Joseph Campbell

Challenges That Arise in Fall

- **Reevaluating** Sometimes just asking the question "What's not working for me?" is the most difficult thing we ever have to do. It's also the first step in making a positive change.
- **Letting Go of Past Structures** To let go of a past identity, especially one that we have been engaged in for a long time, is extremely hard. We would like to believe that it will be easy; if I can just pick this next big thing then it will be a cinch to move on from what I have been doing. We need to find ways to let go of those identities without having the next one already lined up.
- **General Closure** We need to make conscious choices about how to say goodbye to an old structure. How do we close the chapter that we are in now in a way that acknowledges all that we have accomplished *and* what we are leaving behind?
- **Preparing for Uncertainty** If we need to find a whole new vision for an area of our life, we have to plan for the in-between time. We often hear "Don't leave a job until you have another one."

Please don't fall for that message; it is another one of those myths we've been told. When we are shifting to another major direction in our lives we need to honor and accept that it will take time, introspection, and growth to help us get there.

- **Being Aware of Our Feelings** In a world where problem solving is held in high esteem, we need to become more attuned to our emotions. Our feelings are indispensable guides during the transitions in our lives.

*falling leaves
hide the path
so quietly*

*~John Bailey,
Autumn Haiku*

Worksheet: Times I've Been in Fall

It's not uncommon to experience "change amnesia." We feel so overwhelmed by the changes we are encountering that we forget we have been through transitions before, even though they may have been in other parts of our lives and to different degrees.

Since there is no one formula to how this all works, this next exercise asks you to remember some past "Falls" in *your* life, big and small, revisit them, and mine them for useful information to help *you* navigate this transition.

Remember, in Fall we are still in a Life Structure but it no longer fits us. For example, it could be that we just finished working on a project, are a day or two away from returning from a vacation, have left a job or relationship, or are in that last semester of school before graduating.

First, think back and list some of your past Fall experiences. Jot down a word or title that describes it on the lines at the top so you can remember them. As you recall each instance, complete the three sections below by writing down how it felt at the time (Feelings), how that incident helped you personally develop or grow (Gifts), and activities that were useful along the way that enabled you to more gracefully navigate this experience (What Helped).

EXERCISE

Times I've been in...fall

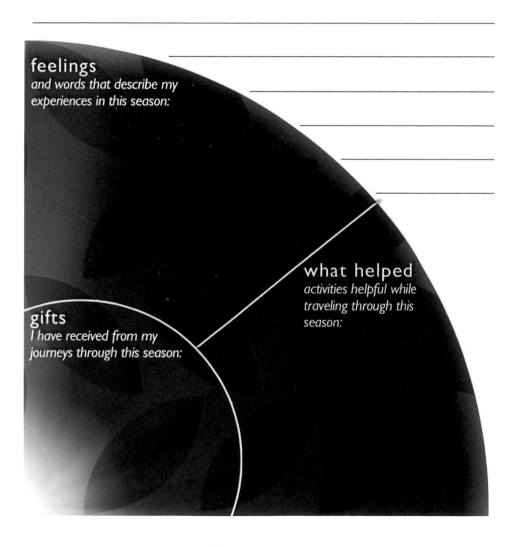

feelings
and words that describe my experiences in this season:

what helped
activities helpful while traveling through this season:

gifts
I have received from my journeys through this season:

FEELINGS

As you complete this section, it's common to describe a range of feelings, some may even appear to contradict each other.

What did you notice and learn about yourself by revisiting your past Fall feelings?

_____

_____

_____

_____

_____

GIFTS

At first we can have a difficult time thinking of any gifts we may have taken away from our Fall experiences. Remember that Thanksgiving happens in the fall, so it's often helpful to think of what we are grateful for from that time. It also takes courage to close out a chapter of our lives. One former client laughed as she was filling out this section. She said: "I never quite thought about it this way before. I received a gift of a great wardrobe from many of the Falls I was in. You see, my avoidance technique was retail therapy!"

What has shifted in you now that you realize the important results that have arisen out of letting go?

_____

_____

_____

_____

_____

Helpful Fall Activities

In addition to the ones you may have listed, here are a few more activities that you may find beneficial in Fall:

FIND PERSPECTIVE

- **Make Time to Step Back** If you notice yourself losing energy, avoiding situations, or feeling angry, use these experiences as clues that you need to slow down and ask yourself some pointed and honest questions.
- **Find New Eyes/Get Insight and Input From Someone Outside the Situation** If it's difficult to find perspective on your own, plan to get help from people whom you trust and who you know will tell you the truth in a supportive way.

SET BOUNDARIES

- **Question Assumptions and Limits** Fall is a time when we feel trapped, stuck, and victimized. Those emotions often stop us from acknowledging that we have any alternatives. Question your assumptions to open up the possibilities for doing things differently from how you previously handled them.
- **Renegotiate Agreements/Responsibilities** What do you need to change to prepare for the upcoming Ending? What Holding Structure can appropriately meet your needs?
- **Pay Attention to Your Own Current Needs** To renegotiate your present situation to fit better, you need to ask yourself some questions: What do you have energy for? How can you begin to build that into what you're involved in right now?

TAKE RESPONSIBILITY

- **Own Your Choices** As much as we are feeling trapped and out of control, we need to realize that blaming others gets us nowhere fast. What new decisions can you make to generate some shifts? What needs to occur for you to realize and accept that the only person ultimately responsible for your experience is you?
- **Define a Short-Term Vision** A vision in Fall is about letting go and closing out a chapter. What is your vision for letting go of whatever aspect of your life is in Fall?

> Then summer fades and passes and October comes. We'll smell smoke then, and feel an unexpected sharpness, a thrill of nervousness, swift elation, a sense of sadness and departure.
>
> *~Thomas Wolfe*

TAKE SMALLER STEPS

- **Develop a Short-Term Plan(s)** It's easy to get overwhelmed when trying to see too far into the future. What plans can you develop that address your immediate needs?
- **Prepare for Closure, Completion** Fall is all about endings. What do you need to put in place to say goodbye to whatever you are engaged in? What rituals can you design that might be helpful to acknowledge your ending and prepare for your unknown next chapter?
- **Move Into Action: Take Steps for Which You Have Energy** You'll hear this a lot throughout this book: energy is always available for the immediate next step. Check in with yourself: what do you have energy for today?

ENGAGE CREATIVITY

- **Brainstorm Alternatives/Think Outside The Box** "If we do what we've always done, we'll get what we've always gotten"—or so the saying goes. Try new strategies for getting unstuck and creating a life you love.
- **Make Changes That Are Within Your Resources and Control** Ask yourself "What do I need/know/want right now?" This will give you the information necessary to take your next, immediate, small step.

Preparing for Winter

Fall gets us ready for the next phase of the cycle, navigating Winter and our Time Between Dreams. Dr. Howard Thurman, 1899–1981, an influential American author, philosopher, theologian, educator, and civil rights leader, summarized Fall in a poetic yet complete way.

For many of us the fall of the year is a time of sadness
and the long memory. All around us there are the evidences of fading,
of withdrawal, of things coming to an end.
What was alive and growing a few short days or weeks ago
seems now to have fulfilled itself and fallen back into the shadows.
Vegetation withers but there is no agony of departure;
there seems to be only death and stillness in the fall.

*It is the time of the changing of the guard. It is the season
of the retreat of energy. It is a time of letting go.
It is the period of the first exhaustion. There is a chill in the air
in the fall. It is not cold; it is chilly, as if the temperature
cannot quite make up its mind. The chill is ominous,
the forerunner of the vital coldness of winter.
But the fall of the year is more than that.
It marks an important change in the cycle of the year.
This change means that summer has past. One season ends
by blending into another. Here is a change of pace
accenting a rhythm in the passing of time. How important this is!
The particular mood inspires recollection and reflection. There is
something very steadying and secure in the awareness that there is an
underlying dependability in life—that change is a part of the experience
of living. It is a reminder of meaning of pause and plateau.
But fall provides something more. There is a harvest,
a time of ingathering, of storing up in nature; there is a harvest,
a time of ingathering, of storing up in the heart. There is the time
when there must be a separation of that which has said its say
and passes—that which ripens and finds its meaning
in sustaining life in other forms. Nothing is lost, nothing disappears;
all things belong, each in its way, to a harmony
and an order which envelops all, which infuses all.
Fall accentuates the goodness of life and finds its truest meaning
in the strength of winter and the breath of spring.*

The Natural Cycles of Change: Winter

"… Each time, I am filled with terror. It doesn't matter that in all my previous hurtles across the void of unknowing I have always made it. I am each time afraid that I will miss, that I will be crushed on unseen rocks in the bottomless chasm between bars. I do it anyway. Perhaps this is the essence of what the mystics call the faith experience. No guarantees, no net, no insurance policy, but you do it anyway because somehow to keep hanging on to that old bar is no longer on the list of alternatives. So, for an eternity that can last a microsecond or a thousand lifetimes, I soar across the dark void of "the past is gone, the future is not yet here."

It's called "transition." I have come to believe that this transition is the only place that real change occurs. I mean real change, not the pseudo-change that only lasts until the next time my old buttons get punched …"

—Danaan Perry, *The Parable of the Trapeze:*
Turning the Fear of Transformation into the Transformation of Fear

APT DESCRIPTIONS OF WINTER include, as the above reading conveys, "the past is gone, the future is not yet here," or the inspiration for the title of this book, *The Time Between Dreams*. Frederic Hudson calls it "cocooning." William Bridges coined it "The Neutral Zone." He authored a landmark book over 30 years ago called *Transitions, Making Sense of Life's Changes*. It delineates three stages of transition: The Ending, The Neutral Zone, and The New Beginning. These stages underscore the need to close out a chapter, then walk through a confusing period before moving on to what's next.

In Chapter 5 on Summer we talked about how the "happily ever after" stories have, throughout childhood and beyond, shaped our perspective on what we should be striving for in life. We know other stories, but we were exposed to them when we were a bit older, so they may not have had the same impact. According to Joseph Campbell, cultures all around the world have mythic stories of the hero's journey. The hero (or heroine) leaves the known, walks into the unknown—the wilderness, oftentimes the underworld—to go fight dragons and emerge from the experience transformed. It's interesting to note the popularity of movie epics such as *Star Wars, Lord of the Rings, The Matrix,* and *Harry Potter.* We've seen these themes arise in older stories too. *The Wizard of Oz* is one film that's aged well and features a female hero. We also know the ancient tales of the Greek myths and the stories about the spiritual mystics.

Transforming Our Personal Dragons

The ultimate dragon is within you.
—Joseph Campbell

Perhaps the fascination with these stories indicates that we are preparing ourselves for our own mythical journeys. Unlike Luke, Frodo, Neo, or Harry, we are not tackling any external wildernesses, but like them and Dorothy, we *are* exploring the internal questions of who we really are and what we need to learn. Confronting our dragons means facing our greatest fears and weaknesses. Only by doing so can we grow into the person we need to become. In this way we are transformed. To transform means to shift our perspective, our paradigm on how we see ourselves and live our lives more intentionally.

This is the hero's journey we each need to embark on through Winter. In doing so we uncover and connect with our true purpose in life. As Joseph Campbell also said: "The adventure of the hero is the adventure of being alive … ."

People say that what we're all seeking is a meaning for life…
I think that what we're really seeking is an experience of being alive,
so that our life experiences on the purely physical plane will have
resonance within our innermost being and reality, so that
we can actually feel the rapture of being alive.

In the Natural Cycles of Change model, Winter is an essential part of this process of coming alive and gives us a kind of roadmap for how we are supposed to get there.

Two Distinct Winter Phases

Winter has two distinct phases, shown by that squiggly, dotted line down the middle of the quandrant. The first phase is an extension of the letting go process. We continue to clear out the old to make room for what's next. Like a snake shedding its skin, it takes time, effort, and doesn't occur all at once. Here we know what we *don't* want but not what we *do* want. We need to find an entirely new vision for whatever area of our lives is in Winter.

In the second phase of Winter we uncover the vision for what we yearn for next. Just as a vision for what we desire in a relationship can't be defined by knowing the person's name, a vision for work isn't the job title or the organization. A vision is a description of what makes you come alive. Later in this chapter we'll go into more detail about how to develop a vision.

The squiggly line is also dotted to indicate a great deal of interchange between the two phases. Remember that this process isn't linear. We flow and cycle through in ways that are not always logical or predictable.

The Old Structure No Longer Works

We can have two reactions to the Ending Point. If we choose it, if we decide that whatever structure we are in no longer fits us, then we typically feel relieved when we finally let go. Whew! We might say to ourselves: "At least the decision is made and I can relax a bit now. The pushing and pulling of Fall is over; I've firmly decided to take the leap and say "no"—this isn't working for me and I'm through with trying to make the former way succeed." That's an enormous, courageous step to take and it's vital that we remember to affirm ourselves as we let go of our old, familiar "trapeze bar."

Shortly after we let go, however, the panic sets in. "Well, it's been a while and I *still* don't know what I want!" We tend to second-guess ourselves and worry that we didn't make the right choice after all. This is normal. When we are in a major transition, we need to remember that it will take some time to work through the process.

If we didn't choose the Ending, for instance, we get laid off with no warning or our partner unexpectedly tells us our long-term relationship is over, our immediate reaction is anger. The structure we were in has ended—it has descended into Winter—but we haven't reached our own internal Ending Point as yet. So we're really still in Fall with the experience. We will have to work through those stages and arrive at our own inner Ending.

You can't depend on your judgment when your imagination is out of focus.
~Mark Twain, 1898

Emptiness and Loneliness

As we enter Winter we've crossed a threshold into the void. We feel empty and lonely. Bear in mind that we've left our previous Life Structure. The loss of identity is huge. Those "props" that have held us up in the past have crumbled; they no longer define who we are. We have now ventured into a Life Transition phase. Connected with that loss of identity is a decrease in our self-esteem. We ask ourselves: "Who *am* I separate from what I *do*?" or "What am I worth when I'm not successful?"

At this juncture, the most difficult thing to do is attend any kind of family or school reunion. You know the drill; at these events people ask questions like "What are you doing now?" or "Who are you with?" We have been joking for many years at Centerpoint that we're going to build an endowment fund by selling tee shirts to people in transition that say: Don't Ask!

Developmental Depression

To pick up where we left off in the Fall chapter regarding Elizabeth Kübler-Ross's stages of grieving—we covered denial, anger, and bargaining—the next element is depression. We define it as a developmental depression, as contrasted with a clinical one, because the sadness and loss is directly related to challenging life events. In clinical depression, this is not always the case and, very simply stated, clinical depression is most often the result of a chemical imbalance in the brain.

The developmental depression experience has two parts: (1) a realization that, both physically and psychologically, we have less energy available. We feel less social and tend to pull back from outside engagements that we normally would have looked forward to. We need to make space for a new dream/vision to rise to the surface of our consciousness. And, (2) we feel fearful. We tend to shut down and not want to face this scary process. While we know we are making room for a new dream, aspects of ourselves still feel too insecure and vulnerable. Those aspects ask, "Am I enough?" and "Is the world big and safe enough for me to really be myself?"

Feelings Are Our Guide

Only by listening to our feelings can we successfully travel though Winter. If our typical way of accomplishing something is to think it through, to use our problem-solving skills and lists of pros and cons, we will feel more and more bogged down and frustrated. Winter isn't an exercise in figuring it out. It's an opportunity to listen more deeply to what needs learning and healing and to transform ourselves into a fuller, more alive person. The word transformation derives from the Greek *metanoia,* which literally translates to "beyond the mind." In other words, we have to feel our emotions and do the grieving.

Dealing with feelings isn't always comfortable. I have to admit that I wasn't as always as agile at facing them as I am today. Another lifetime ago I was living in New York City and extremely frustrated about not being able to find a long-term, permanent relationship. I began therapy to focus on that very question.

As happens frequently in therapy, the issue you think is at the forefront isn't always the real issue. In this case, the difficulty for me was not relationships with others, but my relationship with myself. I had to confront some family of origin issues, and my lack of self-trust. My

Of winter's
lifeless world
each tree
Now seems a
perfect part;
Yet each one
holds summer's
secret
Deep down
within its heart.
~Charles G. State

therapist kept prodding me to listen to and identify my feelings. To put it bluntly, I was resistant. You see, I was a tough New Yorker (born and raised) and if I wanted to deal with something I'd just figure it out and make it happen. It was wimpy to "stay with your feelings."

I was fortunate to have an understanding, patient, and clever therapist; she shared an image/metaphor that has stayed with me for more than 25 years. She asked me to imagine myself at the seashore, in water up to my knees, and facing the sand with my back to the oncoming wave. The wave was of a significant size and she told me that it represents that overwhelming emotion that was threatening to overtake me. She asked: "What would happen to you if you planted your feet firmly and braced yourself against that wave, thinking that you'd be strong and invincible against the onslaught?" My answer was that the wave would crash into me harshly and sharply and I'd most probably get a face full of sand. It would be painful.

Instead, she asked me to envision riding that big wave to shore, allowing myself to flow with it rather than fight against it. As mentioned in the introduction to this book, I'm not a strong swimmer. The thought of taking my feet off the bottom sends me into spasms of panic. It's also a question of control. If I give in and ride that wave to shore then I'm more vulnerable and can't rely on my old way of "toughing" things out. But what if I do? What if I allow myself to ride the wave, that strong emotion? Even though I'd feel out-of-control, I'd have a much smoother ride to shore. The lesson was to allow myself to feel the feelings; that act alone can help me move through them. Uncomfortable? You bet. Necessary? There's no question about it!

Flowing into my emotions and listening to myself has taught me many valuable lessons over the years. I now know that most feelings, while at the minimum unsettling and at the most heartbreaking, aren't going to tow me out into the deep water. I can let them wash over me and pay attention to what they need to teach me. As human beings we are extremely resilient creatures with an amazing capacity to contain a number of conflicting needs and thoughts simultaneously. I am also aware of times when I have to ask for help—and know that it's absolutely essential to do so—and other times when I can rely on my own instincts and resources.

This is Hard Work

You know what? The internal work that we do while traversing each Winter is probably the most challenging endeavor that we ever undertake. And you know what else? We *have* to do it. When we avoid listening to what's below the surface and grieving those things that we've lost and regretted, we limit our ability to live full and contented lives. The struggles that we face in Winter are the experiences that make us stronger in the long run.

Remember Tim from the Fall chapter, the attorney whose life seemed to come crashing down around him? He was impatient and ready to give up. He felt this inner work was a waste of time. He called it "contemplating my navel" and he just wanted to get on with "figuring it all out." He's an extremely bright fellow and if the process was simple, he wouldn't have needed help. In one sense, he had entered into Winter; in another he was still in Fall because he hadn't as yet passed the Ending Point at a deeper emotional level.

In Centerpoint's Passion Search process we ask people to compile a graphical representation of their lives and highlight some of the major peaks and valleys along the way. As they talk about those experiences, they say it is always the valleys, the struggles, the Winters from which they learned the most. No matter how much we wish our greatest lessons could come from the peaks and the delightful times, it never happens that way. We need to confront our growing edge to become the person we were meant to be.

Have you ever heard the story of the cocoon and the butterfly? It's an apt metaphor for the necessity of hard work that's required of us at this stage.

> *Green thoughts emerge from some deep source of stillness which the very fact of winter has released.*
>
> *~Mirabel Osler*

A man found a butterfly cocoon and took it home.
One day a small opening appeared in the cocoon.
He sat and watched the cocoon for several hours as the butterfly
struggled to force its body through that little hole.
Then it seemed to stop making progress. It appeared as if the butterfly
had gotten as far as it could, and it could go no further.
The man decided to help the butterfly in its struggle.
He took a pair of scissors and snipped off the remaining bit of the cocoon...
and the butterfly emerged easily.

As the butterfly emerged, the man was surprised.
It had a swollen body and small, shriveled wings.
He continued to watch the butterfly, expecting that, at any moment,
the wings would dry out, enlarge, and expand to support the swollen body. He
knew that in time the body would contract
and the butterfly would be able to fly. But neither happened.

In fact, the butterfly spent the rest of its life crawling around
with a swollen body and shriveled wings. It was never able to fly.

What the man, in his kindness and haste, didn't understand
was that the restricting cocoon and the difficult struggle
were required for the butterfly to be able to fly.
The butterfly must push its way through the tiny opening
to force the fluid from its body into its wings.
Only by struggling through the opening, can the butterfly's wings
be ready for flight once it emerges from the cocoon.

Sometimes struggles are exactly what we need.
If we went through life without any obstacles, it would cripple us.
We would not be as strong as what we could have been …
And we could never fly.

Being in the Present Moment

An easy way to avoid facing our internal struggles and connecting
with our emotions is to focus on some other time. We erroneously, of
course, reminisce about how perfect things were in the past and thus
get ensnared in our memories. Or we create some great fantasy about
the future and try to live in that flight of our imagination. While it
sounds trite, the more we're not living fully in the present, the more
we will miss what we need to learn. It goes along with that common
phrase, *Life is a journey, not a destination.* There is no future perfect place
to strive toward. This is it.

Always we hope
Someone else has the answer,
Some other place will be better,
Some other time
It will all turn out.

This is it.
No one else has the answer,
No other place will be better,
And it has already turned out.
At the center of your being
You have the answer;
You know who you are
And you know what you want.
There is no need
To run outside
For better seeing.
Nor to peer from a window.
Rather, abide at
The center of your being;
For the more you leave it
The less you learn.
Search your heart
And see
The way to do
Is to be.

—Lao Tzu, translator unknown

This is it. We are exactly where we need to be. Are you feeling any resistance to that thought? That's okay. We've been inundated with many strong messages throughout our lives that there *is* a happily ever after and that life progresses linearly. By questioning those messages we are going against the grain of all we have been taught. If you've gotten this far into this book then you know somewhere down deep inside that you need to live from a different perspective and paradigm. This is not an easy task and it is essential to find the right kind of support along the way to cultivate the conscious life we want to live.

Finding Support in All the Right Places

In many cultures including here in America, many want to avoid this process altogether. How difficult it is to feel vulnerable, out of control, confused, and without direction—and then ask for help in the midst of it all. We do not receive much support for being in Winter. Sometimes it seems we all fall under the spell of what might be referred to as "The Nike Mentality." You know their tagline: "*Just Do It!*" No matter if it's a good fit or whether we have the energy. We're just expected to jump right in and take some kind of action.

At this point the least helpful question friends and family can ask us is, "How many resumes did you send out today?" But ask it, they do. Of course they inquire out of a sense of wanting to be helpful. We have to remember, though, that they are coming from another season's perspective. If one is in Summer, it's challenging to find the patience needed when dealing with someone in Winter. The focus, pace, and priorities are all so different.

In the depth of winter I finally learned that there within me lay an invincible summer.

~Albert Camus

In the summer I have this friend who I am closest to, and sometimes,
in the winter, I long to call her up and say, come here and live with me,
in this cold place. But we are summer friends. There is a rule it seems,
that summer friends don't get together in the wintertime. Now, sitting here,
waiting for her, I realize that I have never seen her in a winter coat,
and for some reason that makes me sadder than anything else in the world.
—Jacqueline Woodson

We need to be selective about whom we ask for support, but we do need to ask for it. This is one of the reasons Centerpoint exists. People find an environment that is nonjudgmental and where they can interact with others who are asking similar questions in their lives. It's not easy to stay on the path of growth when one is doing it alone.

Measuring Winter Activity

With the lack of energy in Winter you might think that everything simply stops. In the season of winter deciduous trees lose their leaves and may look inactive on the surface, but underground the roots are teeming with activity.

January is the quietest month in the garden. ...
But just because it looks quiet doesn't mean that nothing is happening.
The soil, open to the sky, absorbs the pure rainfall while
microorganisms convert tilled-under fodder into usable nutrients

for the next crop of plants. The feasting earthworms tunnel along,
aerating the soil and preparing it to
welcome the seeds and bare roots to come.
—Rosalie Muller Wright

Another metaphor for understanding Winter is pregnancy. It's that time of allowing things to gestate and develop. There's a natural rhythm and timing. No matter how much you want it to be over, wanting is not going to make it so.

It is said that the present is pregnant with the future.
—Voltaire

Yes, quietness and gestation are characteristics of Winter, but that doesn't mean that we do nothing and just wait. It's not simply a fertile void. A great deal of activity occurs but it's different from the undertakings we would tackle in other seasons, and we need to use a different "yardstick" to measure movement.

In Summer we measure movement in external results: How many projects did we complete? What new opportunity arose out of that effort? How many people did we influence? In Winter movement is measured by paying attention to the internal: What new insights came to me today? How do I feel? To what essential information and healing did that feeling lead me? On the surface the answer to these questions may appear trivial, but in Winter these are HUGE steps. We need to acknowledge the almost imperceptible shifts occurring within ourselves. We must listen to our "still, small voice within." Creating an environment that allows us to hear those words is vital. That's why we often find ourselves pulling back from social obligations and embracing our alone time.

The color of springtime is in the flowers, the color of winter is in the imagination.
~Ward Elliot Hour

Back to our attorney, Tim. He decided to attend a Centerpoint four-day retreat to be in an environment where he could examine personal issues he needed to address. While he found himself unable to access his passions and feel introspective during the day, he had some disturbing nighttime dreams. These seemed to open up a new window for him so he could view his transitions from a different perspective. As he talked about these dreams, he sensed that a lot was stirring under the surface. While this felt scary, he also knew he couldn't turn his back on this opening. He had to turn and face what was true for him.

Tim challenged himself to let go of everything with which he previously identified. He confronted some unacknowledged grief and recognized some neglected passions. Tim admits that rather than a waste of time, acknowledging his truth and accepting himself was the most important work he has ever done and the greatest gift he has ever given himself.

Loneliness into Solitude… and the Second Phase of Winter

Life is a series of little deaths out of which life always returns.
~Charles Feidelson, Jr.

Slowly things shift. As we pay more attention to the insights we are gathering about ourselves we find that the emptiness we once felt has morphed into a sense of positive solitude. Instead of a feeling of despair—I'm going to be stuck here forever, nothing is working—we shift into a feeling of hope—things are moving at a proper pace, I'm learning a lot about myself, and I need to do this internal work. In a way we can even acknowledge a feeling of reveling in who we are.

> *Being solitary is being alone well. Being alone luxuriously immersed in doings of our own choice, aware of the fullness of our own presence rather than the absence of others.*
> —Alice Koller

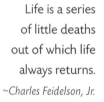

These "doings of our own choice" show up in various forms. Sometimes we go back to an old hobby because the sheer sensation of it would give us pleasure. We don't have any ulterior motives; we don't believe that this is what we will decide to do for the rest of our lives. We start playing that flute again, or dust off the old kiln, or collect rocks just because it would be fun.

We might also find ourselves engaged in some new directions. Friends wonder a little about us when we tell them we're taking an Ethiopian cooking class or writing poetry. Again, these activities aren't "it" for the long run; instead they feed our souls now.

These leisure pursuits help us to reconnect with what we love outside of ourselves and within ourselves. This is the ideal time to begin rediscovering our passion, purpose, and vision. At Centerpoint we call this process Passion Search and offer workshops and services designed around how to get in touch with those things that we want to be sure to build into our next chapter. It's not impossible to think about these questions at other points in the Cycle, but at this phase we feel much more open to possibilities.

Passion Search

The way to find out about happiness is to keep your mind
on those moments when you feel most happy, when you are really happy—
not excited, not just thrilled, but deeply happy.
This requires a little bit of self-analysis.
What is it that makes you happy? Stay with it,
no matter what people tell you.
This is what is called following your bliss.
—Joseph Campbell

While Centerpoint has developed an extensive process on how to uncover and define passion, I'd like to share a macro view of it with you. (The more extensive description will be in the next book.)

centerpoint passion clue gathering process

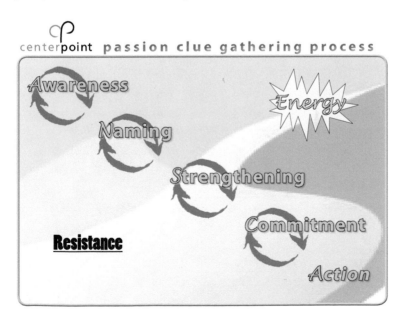

The first step in accessing our dreams involves *Awareness*—noticing those "moments," as Joseph Campbell said, when we are "really happy" in our lives. Since we all tend to be our own worst critics, we often focus on what we don't do well instead of that in which we excel. We need to pay attention to the talents we are aware of now—and throughout our lives—that come naturally and easily to us. Then we have to engage in *Naming* those passions as specifically and clearly as we can. The more specific, the better. Both *Awareness* and *Naming* keep us in our cognitive mode; we need to think about these things to delineate them.

The next two steps are much more experiential. We call them *Strengthening* and *Commitment*. As we become more aware of what we want and can find just the right words to name them, we find that we begin to have a new relationship with them. In *Strengthening* we not only articulate what makes us happy, we actually feel happier as we think and talk about it. The possibilities begin to feel exciting; not only can I do [fill in the blank], I'm good at it and feel proud of that fact.

Commitment is the step of deeply owning that passion/dream. It's when we say to ourselves, "I'm not willing to do without (that passion) in my life." We then take what we know in our hearts and give it a voice so as to describe it, not only to ourselves but to others. We call this a vision statement.

Allow me to share a personal example. When I was attempting to figure out where I wanted to live geographically—I had an acute *Awareness* that New York City was a bad fit for me—I had to find the time and space to step back and dream about the ideal location. It was 1987 and I decided to attend Richard N. Bolles's two-week workshop in Bend, Oregon. Dreaming big enough to describe the perfect place can be quite challenging; I was grateful to have found a supportive environment to help me ask the right questions. It's not always easy to fit this kind of process into our busy day-to-day lives.

Using Bolles's Geographical Chart Exercise, I began to jot down my needs, each one as specific and detailed as humanly possible. While I was trying to imagine my dream location, I had no idea if a place like that even existed. But I kept allowing myself to dream of that ideal city. Here is an example of just how specific we need to be in this *Naming* step.

> "Hear! hear!" screamed the jay from a neighboring tree, where I had heard a tittering for some time, winter has a concentrated and nutty kernel, if you know where to look for it.
>
> ~Henry David Thoreau, 28 November 1858 journal entry

One entry of mine read as follows: *The temperature is between 30 and 90 degrees, it cools off at night in the summers, and has low humidity.* Now that's detailed! It would have been far less useful and much too general to state "I want a temperate climate." That describes way too many options; where would I even begin to explore possible locations?

Another criterion of mine read: *I see mountains and water within the same view.* I can't underscore enough that these statements should be extremely specific and as precise and detailed as possible. With each entry, I found myself getting more and more excited (*Strengthening*). Upon completing the exercise I had a list of about 20 criteria that were essential for me. As I read and reread the description of my new home, it brought tears to my eyes. I didn't know if a place like this existed, but I did know that even if my new setting only fit my top five criteria, I would have been thrilled. Nothing was going to shake my determination to make this happen (*Commitment to my vision*)!

Once I had my vision I couldn't contain my enthusiasm. At that two-week workshop were people who resided all over the world. I started taking *Action*—the next step in this process—by asking people what ideas of geographical locations came to mind as I shared the most important items on my list. I received many suggestions and couldn't wait to begin exploring and researching further. When I eventually found Seattle, I learned in time that it fit *every single one* of my 20 descriptions. Even now, nearly 25 years later, I look around me and know I found my heart's desire. I love this place; I found my life here!

In a way, this manner of defining and articulating our vision is anti-intuitive. Many think that if we keep our needs general and broad we have a better chance of finding something. Well, technically that's true. But the real question is, will it be the best fit? If we "keep our options open," what will we find? Possibly more opportunities quantitatively, but how do you whittle down the numbers and choose among them? You will be spending considerably more time screening out than screening in. The more all-encompassing the description, the more places that description will fit and thus the more difficult it will be to target possibilities and take action. The clearer you can be about describing what brings you alive, the easier it is to find it.

Describing is the key idea here. We have to stay with what we know

> Turn down the noise. Reduce the speed. Be like the somnolent bears, or those other animals that slow down and almost die in the cold season. Let it be the way it is. The magic is there in its power.
>
> ~Henry Mitchell

we need *without* putting a name on it. That makes sense when I was describing where I wanted to live and then needed to connect that description with the place. It also makes sense when we think about a vision for a relationship; we get clear about what characteristics we want in a partner and then know we have to spend some time dating to find a person that fits our needs. So why, when we are drafting a work vision, do we expect to come up with an actual job title? It just doesn't work that way. Again, we need to be able to describe as specifically as possible what we want in an ideal job—our Work Vision statement—and then give ourselves some time to link the description with the position.

For our attorney Tim, this was an entirely different way of looking at things. He always knew he liked to write and that was his impetus for entering law school. Now he understood what it was about writing, what he wanted to contribute with his particular style of writing, as well as his other greatest passions—all in detail. He realized how his choice to go to law school fit into the picture of his life. At this point he was able to appreciate the difficult circumstances that catapulted him into transition. He said, "If all those things in my life hadn't fallen apart, I never would have been able to get to this juncture. I would have missed out on so much."

> If we had no winter, the spring would not be so pleasant: if we did not sometimes taste of adversity, prosperity would not be so welcome.
>
> ~Anne Bradstreet, British poet, 1612-1672

Dreaming Can Be Scary

If, as they say, hindsight is 20/20, then Tim's story is proof. Sometimes it's helpful to hear another's account to know that it is possible to dream big to find our passion and purpose in life. But dreaming can be frightening. Maybe that's because a lot is at stake when we focus on our careers. Or maybe we were brainwashed with some outdated rules about how we're *supposed* to job hunt, i.e., pick a job title, write a resume, send out as many as possible, and hope for the best. But I think it might have something to do with feeling uncomfortable with uncertainty. What's more risky than dreaming and imagining a life of purpose and passion? Children don't find it risky; it's second nature to them to dream and imagine. As adults we so easily get caught up in what's practical and realistic that we end up dismissing the dream even before we begin so we won't be disappointed.

Our dreams are precious things and uncovering them is a vulnerable act. We want assurance that if we allow them to see the light of day, we will be guaranteed of making them real. The problem is that it doesn't work that way. The process involves excavating down deep for all our hidden hopes, passions, and dreams. Then, as they rise into our consciousness, we collect, examine, and clearly name them. We continue to sift through, sorting what's essential to us distinct from what others expect. And, finally, we create a picture of who we are and what we have to give. That's the vision.

Planting Seeds of Vision

We need patience as we allow this process to unfold in a natural progression throughout Winter. It's like planting seeds. Even if we try to speed up their germination time, we still need to protect and nurture them until they are strong enough to grow on their own. One client in Passion Search mentioned that her friend saw her impatience and frustration with the process and told her, "You've planted the seeds. It doesn't do any good to go out there and yell at the lettuce to grow!"

> *In a way Winter is the real Spring*
> *the time when the inner things happen, the resurgence of nature.*
> —Edna O'Brien

Personally, I've gotten to know quite a bit about planting seeds over the past few years. This time I'm not referring to the metaphorical kind. It began when my husband and I renovated our bathroom and installed heating under the tiles. He soon realized that, in addition to making the cats happy, he could also use the floor as a seed incubator to get a head start on the vegetables we would be growing in our summer garden.

Since we have a small bathroom, it gets a bit crowded. Egg cartons with potting soil sheltering tomato, basil, and zucchini seeds cover the tiny floor space. It's dicey walking in there, especially if you have to use the facilities in the middle of the night. Sometimes it seems like nothing is happening; days pass without seeing any growth. It makes

Winter came
down to our
home one night
Quietly
pirouetting
in on silvery-
toed slippers
of snow, And
we, we were
children once
again.

~Bill Morgan, Jr.

you wonder whether they will ever sprout. The one thing that doesn't appear to help is digging them up to spy on their progress.

Gradually, you notice some miniature green specks beginning to displace some of the soil. Then they shoot up quickly, appearing spindly and quite delicate. I have learned, though, that they aren't as fragile as they may look. How did I happen to uncover this interesting tidbit of trivia? There was more than one time that I accidentally stepped on them. I was sure I had destroyed these wee, living creatures. But I didn't. They not only survived, they thrived.

> Winter is not a season, it's an occupation.
>
> ~Sinclair Lewis

Some seeds don't germinate. It can be frustrating. You wait and wait but nothing shows up; no fresh, potential vegetables are going to come from those kernels. At some point you just have to grieve the loss and plant some more.

As I mentioned, my husband likes to get an edge on the growing season, but until—as the seed packages warn—all threat of frost is gone, you can't plant these babies outdoors. Those seedlings mature in our extended kitchen window, then move into the greenhouse for more growth and stability before they get planted in the ground. They need to be nurtured all along the way.

As you can see, this simple experience of planting seeds has taught me some profound life lessons about handling transitions and what I need to do to nurture what's growing in me.

> *From December to March, there are for many of us three gardens—*
> *the garden outdoors, the garden of pots and bowls in the house,*
> *and the garden of the mind's eye.*
> —Katherine S. White

transition structure(s)

Mini-Transition(s) in Winter

We call mini-transitions in Winter, **Transition Structures.** They are temporary choices we make to give ourselves time to step back, to do the work of Winter, and to meet our other immediate needs, financial and otherwise. Some people are able to take sabbaticals or time off; others need to bring in income to pay the rent. Either way, a Transition Structure is not a long-term solution.

Here are a few examples of what people have chosen for Transition Structures. In reality, the possibilities are endless.

- One burned-out secondary school teacher talked in glowing terms about his transition job putting labels on candles. It was flexible, it paid the bills, and he didn't have to talk to anybody.
- A human resources director for a small company was ready to leave her job, but when asked by the president what she needed, she described her ideal, interim position. He realized it was exactly what the company needed so he created a new position for her. And she made more money than in her previous job.
- A therapist going through a personal Winter had no energy or attention available for her clients. She looked around her agency, thought about what she did have energy for, and made a proposal to reorganize their filing system. It was a six-month contract for a certain amount of money; she completed the project in four months and took the last two off.
- Some people elect to remain in their current positions but renegotiate the amount of time spent at the job or their projects so the work doesn't drain them but instead gives them time to Passion Search.
- Others travel, go back to school, or volunteer, not because it will be their next big step, but just because it allows them to grow and learn more about themselves.

> Spring passes and one remembers one's innocence. Summer passes and one remembers one's exuberance. Autumn passes and one remembers one's reverence. Winter passes and one remembers one's perseverance.
>
> ~Yoko Ono

Renewal Point

All the work of Winter leads us to the Renewal Point. As the Summer Positive Plateau is a kind of resting place in the Life Structure and the external world, the Renewal is a resting place in the Life Transition, or in our internal world. We are in no big rush at the Renewal Point because we feel solid and confident in ourselves and our vision.

One word describes people at the Renewal Point—peaceful. While experiencing no less uncertainty and change, our perspective has shifted to one of Acceptance. In a way, this is another Commitment Point. But unlike the Summer Commitment Point, which is a commitment to the external vision, this one is an affirmation to the internal vision of who we are.

A good example of this stage is "Sheila," a young woman who attended an all-day workshop on this cycle. She was there because she hated her job, her boss, and her life in general. One of our Centerpoint staff ran into her a few months later at her place of business, the same place she worked when she attended the workshop. When Sheila saw him, she got excited and yelled out, "I found it!" Our counselor could see that her energy was quite different from what it had been at the workshop and could tell that something had changed for the better. What was different?

She said: "I was running away from being an artist. And *that's who I am!* When I got to that point, everything got easier." Sheila told him that, while she knew what she loved about design, creativity, and art, she was still unclear about what form it was going to take and how she might make a living at it, but she had no doubt that she would. Yes, she was still in the same job but she was no longer miserable. She could see how she was using her design skills and she knew it was a good, temporary choice for her right now. She was ready for Spring and exploring all her possibilities.

Challenges That May Arise in Winter

Each "season" has challenges; these belong to Winter:

- **Loss of identity** We don't know who we are anymore. An identity that we developed in a prior chapter no longer fits and we feel without purpose or direction for that area of our lives. Empty nesters who have had a strong identity of themselves as parents are a common example.

- **Loneliness, solitude** The philosopher/theologian Paul Tillich, 1886–1965, said: "Language… has created the word 'loneliness' to express the pain of being alone. And it has created the word 'solitude' to express the glory of being alone." Winter challenges us to experience and learn from both.

- **Face our fears and embrace the rejected parts of self** This is the ultimate hero's journey and task. Joseph Campbell said: "It is by going down into the abyss that we recover the treasures of life.

Where you stumble, there lies your treasure."

- **Find greater sense of self** We are each unique beings with distinctive combinations of talents, gifts, dreams, upbringings, styles, challenges, and strengths. Winter is our chance to get to know and love ourselves more and to recognize what makes us unique so that we can share these abilities with our families, friends, and the larger community.

We began this chapter with a continuation of *The Parable of the Trapeze* by Danaan Parry. Here is its conclusion:

...I have noticed that, in our culture, this transition zone is looked upon as a "no-thing," a noplace between places.
Sure, the old trapeze bar was real, and that new one coming towards me,
I hope that's real, too. But the void in between? Is that just a scary,
confusing, disorienting nowhere that must be gotten through as fast
and as unconsciously as possible?

NO! What a wasted opportunity that would be.
I have a sneaking suspicion that the transition zone is the only real thing
and the bars are illusions we dream up to avoid the void
where the real change, the real growth, occurs for us.
Whether or not my hunch is true, it remains that the transition zones
in our lives are incredibly rich places. They should be honored, even savored.
Yes, with all the pain and fear and feelings of being out of control
that can (but not necessarily) accompany transitions, they are still
the most alive, most growth-filled, passionate, expansive moments in our lives.

We cannot discover new oceans unless we have the courage
to lose sight of the shore.

—Anonymous

So, transformation of fear may have nothing to do with making fear
go away, but rather with giving ourselves permission to "hang out" in the
transition between trapezes. Transforming our need to grab that new bar,
any bar, is allowing ourselves to dwell in the only place where change really
happens. It can be terrifying. It can also be enlightening in the true sense of
the word. Hurtling through the void, we just may learn how to fly.

There is a privacy about it which no other season gives you ... In spring, summer and fall people sort of have an open season on each other; only in the winter, in the country, can you have longer, quiet stretches when you can savor belonging to yourself.

~Ruth Stout

Worksheet: Times I've Been in Winter

It's essential to remember that we have been in the Time Between Dreams at various points in our lives, in big and little ways. It is helpful to recall them so we can know why it's worth doing this hard work and what helped us allow the path to unfold. In Winter we've let go of making the old thing work and know what we don't want, not what we do want.

Please recall and list some of your past Winter experiences. Jot down a word or title that describes it on the lines that follow so you can remember them. As you recall each instance, complete the three sections on the next page by writing down how it felt at the time (Feelings), how that incident helped you personally develop or grow (Gifts), and activities that were useful along the way that enabled you to more gracefully navigate this experience (What Helped).

Have you ever noticed a tree standing naked against the sky,
How beautiful it is?
All its branches are outlined, and in its nakedness
There is a poem, there is a song.
Every leaf is gone and it is waiting for the spring.
When the spring comes, it again fills the tree with
The music of many leaves,
Which in due season fall and are blown away.
And this is the way of life.

~Krishnamurti

EXERCISE

Times I've been in...winter

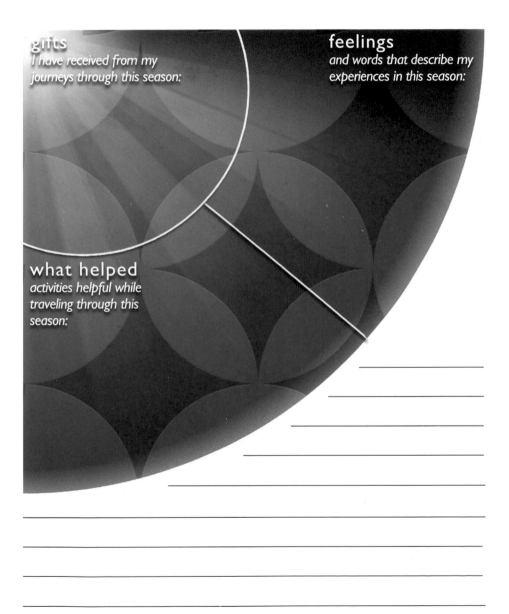

gifts
I have received from my
journeys through this season:

feelings
and words that describe my
experiences in this season:

what helped
activities helpful while
traveling through this
season:

FEELINGS

As you complete this section, it's common to uncover a range of feelings, some even appear to contradict each other.

What did you notice and learn about yourself by revisiting your past Winter feelings?

_____

I prefer
winter and   _____
fall, when you
feel the bone   _____
structure of the
landscape the   _____
loneliness of it,
the dead feeling _____

GIFTS
of winter.
Something
waits beneath it,
the whole story
doesn't show.
~Andrew Wyeth

At first it can be difficult recalling any gifts gained from our Winter experiences. Remember back to the internal activity of Winter. Gifts might include a deepened sense of self-knowledge, confidence, or worth. Revisit the awesomeness of the winter season and the amazing, natural rhythm of nature. Perhaps one of your major gifts is something as simple as rest and renewal. And, don't forget that it is in Winter that we all reconnect with our sense of passion, purpose, and vision.

What has shifted in you now that you realize the important results that have arisen out of letting go?

_____

_____

_____

_____

_____

Helpful Winter Activities

In addition to the ones you may have listed on page 92, here are a few more activities that you may find useful in Winter:

STEP BACK TO ALLOW TIME, SPACE, AND FOCUS FOR REFLECTION AND INTROSPECTION

- **Create an Interim Plan to Allow Enough Safety for Stepping Back** If you are worried about how you will pay the rent or buy food, you won't have enough bandwidth for healing, growth, and passion searching. If you can take a sabbatical, a leave, or not work at all, take advantage of the time. If not, you may need to take a transition job that would, at the minimum, not drain you and, at its best, you would find enjoyable.

- **Avoid Major Commitments** This may not be the best time to plan a move across country, or a wedding, or that next big career move. Remember, you have less energy and no clear vision for whatever part(s) of your life is (are) in transition. Any big step will sap your energy even more.

- **Minimize Expenses and Demands** Make a budget and figure out just how little you can live on. If you live beyond your means you will just create more stress for yourself. Simplify the demands on your life in every way possible. This is not the time to try to save for your retirement. Remember, winter is not a "climbing the ladder" time. And, also remember that downsizing in this way is a temporary, interim choice. You won't get stuck in whatever transition structure you've set up for yourself if you go into it consciously and with a clear intention.

- **Sit with the Uncertainty Without Jumping Ahead** Give yourself permission *not* to know. Embrace the time between dreams as a necessary part of your life transformation.

TAKE SMALLER STEPS

- **Develop a Short-Term Plan** While the uncertainty of Winter encourages us to "go with the flow," some of us find that having a sketch of how to proceed through this season is reassuring. How much time is this Winter requiring? Three months? Six months? A year or two, or more? The parameters directly relate to how

> For the unlearned, old age is winter; for the learned it is the season of the harvest.
>
> ~*The Talmud*

big the transition is. Then divide that overall period into smaller time frames: What do you desire this week, this month? And please remember that we must always be ready to revisit the plan at any time to revise and redirect it, by listening to our internal needs along the way.

- **Take Steps for Which You Have Energy** Energy is always available for our next immediate step. However our "shoulds" tend to get in our way. For example, you may be exhausted and have energy for a nap but another voice says that would be a waste of time and you *should* keep busy working on these issues. Unless you get the rest that you require, you won't have energy for any subsequent steps. Stop fighting your gut. Go with what it knows is essential.

FIND A NEW VISION

- **Take Stock and Value Your Personal Talents and Gifts** Apart from trying to figure out what it all means or what you are going to do, begin to collect your passion clues—all your clues. What comes so naturally to you that you discount it? When you are having fun and losing all track of time, notice what is in place. Ask your family and friends what they think your greatest talents are. Go through a passion search process on your own, with a book, with a career counselor, or with others.
- **Summarize the Vision and the Essence of What You Want and Need** Define your mission statement, clearly and concisely. Without naming any particular job title or form that the vision might take, describe your dream.

Spring Forward

The work of Winter is necessary to lay the foundation for what's next. As we commit to our vision, our energy returns.

Every gardener knows that under the cloak of winter
lies a miracle ... a seed waiting to sprout, a bulb opening to the light,
a bud straining to unfurl. And the anticipation nurtures our dream.
—Barbara Winkler

The Natural Cycles of Change: Spring

Spring won't let me stay in this house any longer!
I must get out and breathe the air deeply again.
—Gustav Mahler, composer and conductor, 1860–1911

Spring is nature's way of saying, "Let's party!"
—Robin Williams, actor and comedian, 1951–

Bridging the Gap

OVERALL, SPRING ACTS as a bridge between who we are—our internal vision—and the external form the vision will embody. It's a time to explore, experiment, try things on, and test things out. We are coaxed out of our cocoon to discover and connect with others who share our enthusiasms.

A variety of roads leads to any destination, so we can traverse many different "bridges" that will guide us in the direction of our dreams. Spring is the "season" when we uncover creative ways to get what we want.

Energy Returns

At the Renewal Point, our energy returns. It's like pouring liquid into a glass; the energy fills and fills until it has no other choice but to over-flow. We can no longer stem the tide. We feel compelled to share our passions and are excited about the possibilities.

Mark Twain referred to this experience when he said,

It's spring fever....And when you've got it, you want—
oh, you don't quite know what it is you do want, but it just fairly
makes your heart ache, you want it so!

Here we have the heart of our vision: a description of what's alive in us, what we want to contribute, and what we need. What we don't have—and can't really know at this point—is the form that the vision will take. Unlike during Fall and Winter, in Spring we are now ready to tap into this new energy and uncover the opportunities that await us.

renewal

Vision as Compass

The vision is our compass and guides us in our decision-making. With a specific and solid compass, we can evaluate every opportunity that arises and compare it with what we know we need. In the previous chapter I related my story of finding Seattle. My list of 20 clear and detailed criteria was the vision, the dream, the ideal, for what was perfect for me in a new place to live. While it took some time to research cities that fit what I needed—these were pre-Google days—I had no doubts when I found it. And, any time I had butterflies about moving clear across country and changing my entire life, I could easily refer back to my vision to remember why Seattle was such a perfect fit. Our vision keeps us on track as we begin exploring what exists in the world that matches up with what we desire.

> Any life career that you choose in following your bliss should be chosen with that sense—that nobody can frighten me off from this thing. And no matter what happens, this is the validation of my life and action.
>
> ~Joseph Campbell

What a WorkVision Isn't

Standard explanations about how the job search process works have been drilled into our brains, and now we must shed the old rules and embrace a new twenty-first century approach. Even after clients at Centerpoint have learned our creative method for making a life worth living, we still see this outdated mindset pop up time and again. It is so ingrained in society that it's often difficult to let go of the notion that a WorkVision is *not* a job title. That notion is the greatest impediment to finding our fit. As described in the Winter chapter, a vision is a description of what makes you come alive. Yes, it's defined as specifically as possible, but one vision can lead to many diverse options.

The heart of my vision is to assist adults who are facing developmentally difficult times in their lives, those we all run up against in the normal course of our human existence. I am called to accompany them and provide resources and perspective on their journeys toward learning and growth. As you can probably guess, my work and the way that I am doing it fits my vision perfectly. But this isn't the only job that would fit me.

I remember as a teenager being fascinated with a particular career path. I wasn't sure what it was that drew me and didn't tell anyone about it at the time, probably because I didn't want to upset my friends and relatives. In hindsight, I can see that this particular path would have been a good choice for me because it would have been a match for my vision. What was this odd occupation I considered? Undertaker. Think about it. The way that I would perform this job would not be focused on embalming dead bodies. I would be assisting the people who were grieving losses in their lives so that they could learn and grow from those experiences.

At the outset you might not think of this vocation as similar to my work now. That's why it is so imperative not to begin the exploration process with a focus on job titles. Besides, who knows what jobs will be needed next month or next year? The world is changing so rapidly that, if we can stay with the vision, then we can expand our possibilities.

Exploring Is a Creative Process

If you can see your path laid out in front of you step by step,
you know it's not your path. Your own path you make
with every step you take. That's why it's your path.
—Joseph Campbell

Exploring begins internally and each step you take boosts energy, ideas, and inspiration for the next step. It is dynamic, alive, and evolving. It absorbs information and excitement, transforming them into new ideas and configurations over and over again.

Exploring is a dynamic process between the internal "What do I want?" "What's going on inside?" and the external "What's out there in the world that's a good fit?" It allows you to take a next, small, immediate step by testing and acting. This step then leads to gathering more information to incorporate internally, and so on. There is no place anywhere in the cycle for a linear process—even in Spring.

As an example and to follow up on our relationships analogy, when you have a vision of the characteristics you want in a partner, you can't expect his/her name to simply pop into your mind. Or, you can't just sit at home and wait for that perfect person to ring your doorbell or show up on an Internet matching site. You've got to go out and date, usually for quite a while. As you meet more people, you integrate what works and doesn't work for you into your idea, your vision for your life partner. Unless you are the luckiest person in the world, it will take some time to meet the person who is right for you.

Dating involves persistence—persistence to keep at it, even going out with someone who, on the surface, might not seem like a fit. This also happens with careers and jobs. If you are in a transition with your work you probably are reading this book because you are not looking for just any fit, you want the right fit—one with purpose and meaning. Often, this goal is a departure from the form that your work has taken in the past. The traditional methods of searching won't work; you can't just post your resume online and wait for the offers to come rushing in. You have to develop more creative strategies to uncover the opportunity that's just right for you.

You might wish to skip this phase, but that is not possible. It would be like wishing for Spring to follow Summer or Fall; in the natural order, no amount of hoping will make it so. An old proverb that states, *No matter how long the winter, spring is sure to follow.* Taking the time to explore and experiment is an essential step for finding what you need. Allowing it to unfold in its own graceful—and sometimes confusing—way is the only way to traverse this season.

Spring Is a Disorderly Season

This chapter was especially difficult to write. For the longest spell, I couldn't imagine why. It eventually dawned on me. Being a creative time, Spring progresses in a less-than-orderly manner. How was I to describe this process in a way that would make sense to a reader?

Luckily, my memory was jogged about my friend Rhonda's spring cleaning ritual. She takes everything out of her closets and cupboards that she wants to recycle, re-order, or retain. She deposits these items all over her house in piles that look unruly and untidy to anyone else's eye. It's so chaotic that her husband, upon entering the house, imagines a tornado must have somehow materialized indoors. But Rhonda has her own system and, by the end of the project, the piles are gone and the house is organized in a way that works much better for her.

If this chapter feels somewhat higgledy-piggledy to you, sometimes feeling scattered, disorganized, or repetitive, please understand that this is exactly how Spring unfolds. While we all yearn for a plan with precise rules, formulae, and a step-by-step procedure to follow, we need to embrace the messiness of this season and concoct creative methods for finding our fit.

"Creative" Spring Stories

Since exploring is, at its heart, a creative process, you can learn a lot from your past resourceful experiences. These experiences offer encouragement and remind you of your unique "creative" style and approach to working with obstacles that may arise along the way.

For the purposes of this exercise, expand the definition of the word "creative" to include any of your experiences that meets these criteria:

1. You had some need, wish, or desire
2. that went through a process
3. and that ultimately resulted in finding a satisfactory fit or expression in the world for that original desire

While this process can include any kind of artistic, literary, or musical creative activity, it applies equally to other experiences that you may not perceive as creative. Some examples might include:

- finding an intimate relationship that fits you
- choosing a neighborhood to live in, a school to go to, etc.
- finding a new pet, or a good auto mechanic, or a satisfying friendship

- finding a gift for someone that was "just what you were looking for"
- redecorating a room in your house or landscaping the yard
- planning a trip, putting together an event or party, solving a problem as part of a team

EXERCISE

From the definition and examples above, make a list of your past creative experiences that come to mind. Allow yourself to include both major and fairly minor events. Then choose one (1) experience from your list where:

- The ultimate result was especially satisfying *and*
- The path from your original desire to a satisfactory fit in the world was circuitous with lots of twists and turns that you could not have easily guessed about or mapped out before you began.

IF COMPLETING THE EXERCISE ON YOUR OWN:

1. Think about the experience. What were the active steps you took to reach your desired outcome?
2. Make some notes, using the Spring quadrant on facing page, to describe the elements present. How did new information, options, or resources arise that could not have logically been planned?
3. Feel free to choose another experience (or even several of them) from your list that fits the same criteria above and repeat steps 1 and 2, again jotting down the elements that you notice.
4. Review your notes. What are the patterns you notice around how you were able to get what you needed?

IF COMPLETING THE EXERCISE WITH ANOTHER:

- Tell the story to your partner. What were the active steps you took to reach your desired outcome?
- Your partner, while also probing your story for specifics, takes note of the elements detected. (Use the Spring quadrant on the facing page, if you like, for your notes.) How did new information, options, or resources arise that could not have logically been planned?
- From the story you told and the one that you heard, discuss with each other the elements that made it possible to reach these goals.

> The ultimate aim of the quest must be neither release nor ecstasy for oneself, but the wisdom and the power to serve others.
>
> ~Joseph Campbell

Now review the list of elements that arose from this creative stories exercise. Surprise! You already know how to get what you want in life. Even though we only focused on small, manageable things like finding the right gift for someone, the steps are *exactly the same* as they would be for attaining larger goals. Let's now outline some overall, fundamental tenets to remember throughout Spring.

No winter lasts forever; no spring skips its turn.

~Hal Borland

Always Return to the Inspiration

Creativity always begins on the inside. The first question is always *"What do I most desire right now?"* Inspiration emanates from the energy you have for what you need. The creative process is organic. It revolves around inspiration. Anytime we get off track, we must always come back to this essential question.

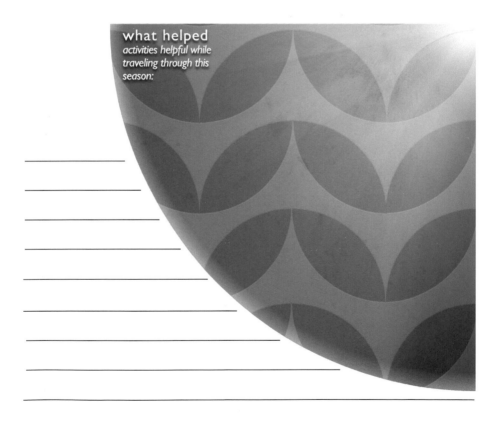

what helped
activities helpful while traveling through this season:

In pursuing our grander, loftier dream, the inspiration is our vision statement. Revisiting the vision is what keeps us on track over time as we experience the ups and downs of the exploring process. All explorers need to refer to the compass every so often to keep on track.

It was one of those March days when the sun shines hot and the wind blows cold: when it is summer in the light, and winter in the shade.

~Charles Dickens

For as long as she can remember, Sandy had been interested in psychology and the ability of people to change their lives by changing their perspectives and beliefs. Along the way, however, her clarity was muddied by a father who told her she was nuts. She took to heart the messages of "you can't make a living at that" and "you're not cut out for that type of work." These statements completely derailed her passion so she discarded the idea. At age 46 she was jarred awake by a combination of working in so many uninteresting jobs that she couldn't even keep count—and a traumatic divorce. Sandy realized she had no time to lose. She was determined and committed to figuring out her life's purpose.

One of her biggest passions has been her own life-long journey on the winding road toward happiness and self-awareness. Sharing her life lessons, insights, and knowledge to help others has been her unspoken career since as far back as she can remember. Now she was ready to explore how to do that. Sandy began the exploration process with the question "What is out there that connects my fascination in psychology and helping people heal their lives?" Of the answers she uncovered, the one that spoke to her heart was becoming a transpersonal counselor. What credentials would she need to move in this direction?

In her research she found a local university program that sounded as though it was designed just for her. Her enthusiasm for applying waned a bit when she learned that the deadline for that year's entrance had passed. But she wasn't going to let that stand in her way. She explored creative strategies to connect with people at the university who might be able to put in a good word for her. They did and she excitedly waited to hear about her admission.

When she didn't get in, disappointment took hold of her. Sandy questioned the viability of this direction. She stepped back again to ask creative questions about how else she could live her vision of helping others change their lives. Remember that the vision is the compass we use to make sure we remain on the right path for us.

But fear can seep in at any time, often when we least expect it. Sandy began to realize that becoming a counselor also meant thousands of hours of intern supervision, perhaps even unpaid hours. Then there was the required licensing exam. If she didn't pass, she would have to wait another year to retake it. This approach was adding up to a lot of time: two years in academia, two more years of supervision, and a possible fifth year if she failed the licensing exam. She was going into debt to pay for schooling; how could she pay that back and then not make money while interning? And, she would be over 50 before she was able to begin a counseling practice. The barriers and obstacles seemed overwhelming. Maybe she should cut back the dream, let go of enrolling in a masters psychology program, and instead focus on a shorter, less involved course in coaching?

As she explored coaching possibilities, something was not sitting well with her, she felt less and less energized overall. While investigating this avenue, she realized that she was compromising and that coaching wouldn't be enough for her—and then she knew what she had to do. After more inquiry into holistic counseling programs, her enthusiasm began to return again. Sandy's confusion was a signal that reinforced her own inner wisdom—she simply needed to take the steps to begin down the path to becoming a counselor. Yes, she would be over 50 when she finished studying; yes, she would be in debt; and yes, it might take three or four years before she could establish her career, but she loved this new direction. This was her inspiration and what her heart desired. Nothing could deter her from this choice.

As this example once again illustrates, Spring is not a linear process. Following the compass of passion takes us through a multitude of twists and turns leading us toward the path of purpose.

Generate Ideas

Take your vision statement and generate as many ideas as possible from it. Brainstorm without boundaries. One method is to dissect your vision into its specific "ingredients" to create a brainstorming "recipe." If you want to brainstorm possible work directions, the exercise on the following page may help:

Career Brainstorming Recipe

Use playfulness as a source of creative ideas. Have a party! Many have found it extremely helpful to bring together friends and acquaintances to generate ideas for the structure their vision might take. Share your key ingredients below and let the group go wild; no idea is too outrageous. Ask them to describe the work instead of naming a job title. Ensure that people aren't only making guesses based on what might be realistic or practical. The sky's the limit. Ideas don't even need to

ESSENTIAL INGREDIENTS

List three or four elements that you know are essential for your career fulfillment. These are the key puzzle pieces that you need and that are non-negotiable for your work satisfaction.

ADDED VALUE INGREDIENTS

List whatever comes to mind that are areas of knowledge, experience, skill, or natural aptitude even if they don't need to be a part of your work.

ENERGY INGREDIENTS

List what you have energy for. Include things like your areas of passion, great interest, and special fascination; the populations you want to work with and on behalf of; favorite hobbies, etc. Include what needs to be in your life even though it doesn't necessarily have to be a part of your work.

be legal at this juncture. Your role is to jot down every notion without editing or thinking about why it *isn't* possible. Quantity is more important than quality.

Afterwards your job is to sort through all the brainstorms and highlight those that catch your attention and feel exciting or interesting, even if you don't know all that they entail. The next step is to learn more about those ideas that grabbed you.

Questions Are Your Guide

Idea generation is one step. More importantly, focus on the energy they bring. Be curious and allow that energy to carry you further into the unknown. Create questions from your ideas that lead toward a path for action. These questions tend to begin with *"How can I"* and *"Who else is."* For example:

- *How can I find a way to bring together my passion for painting large murals and my need to be of service?* or
- *Who else is bringing together developmentally disabled children and horses to build self-esteem and independence?* or
- *How can I downsize my life so that I can have both time and money in retirement?*

If you realize that your questions begin with *"Can I?"* or your brain is telling you these ideas aren't even possible, then you have simply uncovered another clue in the process. You need to step back into Winter to gain confidence and clarify your vision.

From your creative questions, commit to taking the very next step:

- With whom can you talk about this matter?
- What do you need to do that?
- What action(s) can you take to meet that need?
- Follow the energy, listening and improvising all along the way.
- Pay attention to the synchronicity that naturally shows up.

Synchronicity

Follow your bliss.
If you do follow your bliss,
you put yourself on a kind of track

that has been there all the while waiting for you,
and the life you ought to be living is the one you are living.
When you can see that,
you begin to meet people
who are in the field of your bliss,
and they open the doors to you.
I say, follow your bliss and don't be afraid,
and doors will open where you didn't know they were going to be.
If you follow your bliss,
doors will open for you that wouldn't have opened for anyone else.

—Joseph Campbell

In the spring I have counted one hundred and thirty-six different kinds of weather inside of four and twenty hours.

~Mark Twain

This passage is such a wonderful description of synchronicity. Carl Jung originally coined this term and defined it this way: *Synchronicity is the coming together of inner and outer events in a way that cannot be explained by cause and effect and that is meaningful to the observer.* It is making meaning out of coincidence. He calls synchronicity "a causal connecting principle" linking mind and matter.

An interesting story and widely shared story about Jung involves one of his clients, a woman who was extremely rational, with stock answers for all his questions. She also was resistant to expressing feelings. Jung wrote:

I was sitting opposite her one day with my back to the window,
listening to her flow of rhetoric. She had an impressive dream the night before,
in which someone had given her a golden scarab—a costly piece of jewelry.

While she was still telling me this dream, I heard something
behind me gently tapping on the window. I turned around
and saw that it was a fairly large flying insect that was knocking
against the windowpane from outside in the obvious effort
to get into the dark room. This seemed to me very strange.
I opened the window immediately and caught the insect in the air
as it flew in. It was a scarabaeid beetle, whose gold-green color
most nearly resembles that of a golden scarab. I handed the beetle
to my patient with the words, 'Here is your scarab.' The experience
punctured the desired hole in her rationalism and
broke the ice of her intellectual resistance.

Synchronicity describes the experience that occurs when we are on the right path—we feel extremely lucky. Things happen that we could not have planned. As I mentioned in the Summer Mini-Transitions story of my career path, a reasonably priced apartment showed up just as I was considering my first career development position, and I met a person in a most unusual place who told me about a job opening that shaped the second phase of my career and my life. Other instances abound.

Centerpoint's vision was to be located on a site in Seattle, surrounded by nature, where clients could find peace and a stress-free environment to do their transition work. Oh, yes, and with free, ample parking too. For the first 12 years we rented office space in downtown Seattle because we just didn't see how it could be possible for us to find that ideal setting. We stayed with a smaller vision, one we thought was logical.

At the end of our lease and about to renegotiate a new one, I presented the situation to the board members. Because every nonprofit board meeting is always focused on how to save or make money, and since it was a buyer's market at the time, I had the idea to negotiate several months of free rent into our new lease. The board thought this idea was good and one member suggested I speak with her brother, a commercial real estate agent who specialized in assisting nonprofits. He could give me some concrete facts from which to work.

When I called he asked me to describe the space that would be ideal for Centerpoint. That was easy! I shared our vision as outlined above, not expecting to find it; I was just doing research so we could save some money. It turned into a perfect example of synchronicity. This real estate agent had just been hired to find small nonprofit tenants for the Talaris Campus, 18 acres of green in Seattle, with lots of free parking. This location is a hidden treasure; many native Seattlelites don't even know it exists. We jumped at the chance to create our next growth step for Centerpoint and fulfill our vision, even though that wasn't the original plan. Nine years later we remain on the campus in an idyllic setting for our work.

Synchronicity requires a commitment and clarity to one's vision, being open to creative ideas, and an ability to shift gears midstream to

Spring is when you feel like whistling even with a shoe full of slush.

~Doug Larson

walk the path of possibility. There are various styles of being creative and open. What's yours?

Acknowledge Your Personal Creative Style

Discover and recognize your own creative style and use it to build energy and momentum. Each of us has a preferred style—the one that we express most in the world—of how we engage this resourceful process. We can also access and use other creative styles as we learn what's needed for action.

Our unique creative styles appear in different forms at different times, and for various purposes. On the chart at right, highlight or circle all that sound like you...

Next, go back through the chart and ask which of the above, that may not be your natural style, would be useful to build into your repertoire as you explore your options? What next step are you ready to take today?

Feel the Flow

The term "flow" was introduced into the mainstream by Mihály Csíkszentmihályi in his book, *Flow: The Psychology of Optimal Experience,* published in 1990. We all have at one time or another experienced this phenomenon. Think of times when, while focusing on an activity, you've lost all track of time.

This experience has occurred to me so often while writing this book. Sitting at the computer I find myself immersed in the information I want to pass along to you, the reader. I check the clock thinking I've been at it for 30 minutes. Instead, hours have passed. I have no idea where they've gone.

Musicians, athletes, gamers, those who meditate, just to name a few examples, often find themselves in the state of flow. As someone who is in Spring and figuring out how to make your dream a reality, pay attention to those encounters with flow.

- Recognize and allow flow of your energy and styles.
- Tune into "flow" moments; learn from them and integrate them at each step along the way.

	ACTIVE STYLE	COGNITIVE STYLE	OUTWARD STYLE	INTERNAL STYLE
What I say to myself:	I won't know until I try. How will I really know until I test it out?	If I don't have the answer, I am doing something wrong.	I gain clarity and feel good by talking about things.	I like to spend time reflecting and focusing on personal growth.
Credo I live by:	Taking action and doing something is the most important thing in life.	I see myself as a student of my own interests and curiosity; questions lead the way.	Live in the moment and focus on the here and now.	Live from the inside out; create one's own reality and trust one's intuition.
My learning style:	I learn by jumping into action, both feet first.	I learn by stepping back and uncovering the facts needed to figure things out.	I learn by talking out loud.	I learn by asking difficult questions of and listening to myself.
Blocks arise when:	I get ahead of myself and find I'm committed to something I'm not excited about.	I focus solely on getting the answer, the conclusion, and waiting for that "aha" moment.	Externalizing is difficult to do when I get negative feedback from others.	I get stuck in my internal process and find it difficult to act.
What helps:	Consciously choosing smaller and slower steps; confirming the new vision has all of what I need before committing to it.	Taking small steps based on what I know at each point along the way and before I have all the final answers.	Finding the right, supportive people to talk with and engaging in activities that help me trust myself.	Creating a healthy balance of external action with internal processing.

Welcome Blocks

Obstacles will undoubtedly arise as you proceed. Not only expect them, but welcome them with open arms. Blocks are there for several beneficial reasons:

1. **Course Corrections** As we saw in completing the Creative Stories exercise, running up against closed doors is just as helpful in getting you where you want to be as encountering synchronicity. Receiving messages of *no, you can't do that* or *that isn't needed* forces you to ask creative questions like *Who do you know who has done something everyone told them was impossible?* or *What are the challenges that haven't as yet been addressed in this field?* You will

be amazed at how often obstacles can lead to the knowledge of something that you didn't previously know existed.

2. **Mistakes and Roadblocks Can Lead to the Most Promising Discoveries** When scientists describe how they discover solutions to sticky problems, they frequently say that it was an error of some sort that lead them to the awareness of what was needed. Without that gaffe, they wouldn't have been able to untangle the puzzle in front of them. If you, for example, find yourself in a conversation with someone who doesn't have an inkling about your area of interest, don't just walk away. Instead, fire up your curiosity, ask lots of questions, and find areas of commonality. It may just lead to a road you didn't even know was there.

3. **Slow Down, You're Moving Too Fast** Besides being a great line from a Simon & Garfunkel song, the message is essential. At times, obstacles act like stop signs. How can you incorporate some pausing time for revisiting the vision and reconnecting with the passion that underlies your vision? By stopping to listen, new insights will surface so you can perceive the situation with new, fresh eyes.

Creative T-e-n-s-i-o-n

The tension between your vision and reality can be both scary and exciting. It is a natural tension to feel but it's also a tricky balancing act; you must hold your ideal, pie-in-the-sky dream while, at the same time, explore options in the real, rough and tumble world. Vision and reality may appear to be at odds with each other; you may be tempted to focus on just one or the other. Be aware when you feel as though the situation has become an either/or proposition. Your quest is not to cut the dream down to fit within the bounds of reality or into what is practical. And, it's not hanging on so tightly to a particular and ideal form for the vision that you eliminate viable possibilities. Use the tension as energy and inspiration.

From Fall Through Winter Into Spring

"Orlando," a fifth-year associate attorney in an insurance defense law firm, was miserable. He had thought for a while about finding a new direction, but inertia kept him stuck where he was. That is, of course, until he was fired. Unlike our other lawyer, Tim, whose story was told in Winter, Orlando was ecstatic about the news. It gave him the boot that he needed to make a bigger change.

In planning his transition, Orlando decided that he needed time to define his vision. He had always followed others' expectations of him—his family, wife, and friends—and was now ready to figure out who he was and what he wanted. We talked about designing a transition structure, where he could work at an interim job that wasn't taxing or draining him. He decided, however, to take time off; he was afraid that his over-achieving personality would cause him to immerse himself, even in something that might be part time or way below his aptitudes.

He arranged matters with his wife; they had to manage the mortgage, the two kids, and her role as a stay-at-home mom. They developed a temporary plan that was successful for them: cutting down expenses and her going back to work part-time.

Orlando went on a roller coaster ride through Winter. Some days it was difficult even to get out of bed, feeling like he wasn't worthy enough to create a life that he loved. Other days he found he had a little more hope, energy, and confidence, learning about himself and building his self-esteem. As he progressed through the Passion Search process, he reconnected with his natural talents and got to know and value himself more.

For Orlando, Winter lasted about nine months. We both could see the shifts in him as he more clearly defined his vision. When we started brainstorming ideas from his WorkVision statement, he could definitively say "yes" and "no" to certain things. He wanted to work with individuals and information in "this way" but not "that way." That clarity was a huge clue that he was in Spring. His energy had returned and he could sort through ideas and options without getting pulled off course.

If he had instead said things like, *"Yes, but, that wouldn't work because…"* we would know for certain that he was still in Winter. The "yes, buts" are a sure sign of it. There is a wisdom that people have in Winter; when you give them options, something down deep inside

Behold, my friends, the spring is come; the earth has gladly received the embraces of the sun, and we shall soon see the results of their love!

~Sitting Bull

knows they aren't ready and they will come up with every reason why things won't work out. The wise part is afraid that they will again get trapped into something that isn't a fit.

This vacillation is like later winter when the weather begins to turn and, wow, some days sure do resemble spring. In our optimism we want to go out and put flowering plants in the ground. But if it's too soon, the cold weather will surely return and our newly planted buds will freeze. There is no way to rush the seasons. We continually need to listen to ourselves to know when the time is right to sow.

The time was right for Orlando. He developed a strategy; he was excited about exploring several industries. They included high school or college sports coaching and other related areas, such as finding a way to connect high school athletes with appropriate colleges. He also was interested in some areas related to the law such as arbitration and labor unions, and kept practicing law in a firm on his list. That last one was there, he said, because he just wanted to make sure that he was going to rule that option out.

He began the information gathering process and started networking with people who could give him more data about the needs that existed in each of those areas. He came back for an appointment and said gleefully: *"I know what I want to be. I want to be a professional interviewee because I'm having so much fun!"* His meetings were going well and he was learning much about how he could make a difference. He was also hearing about positions in the hidden job market.

But what he eventually did and how he found it is a perfect Spring synchronistic story. Part of his daily ritual in Winter was to visit the gym and work out. He really enjoyed it, it gave some structure to his week, and helped him get going in the morning, especially on those days when he had little motivation to get out of bed. One day, in the midst of his exploring, he was at the gym. Orlando noticed a guy who had a similar gym schedule to his, but they had never talked. Then, one day this gentleman approached him. He told Orlando that while he had observed him over the past months, he now found himself curious about why he was there so frequently. Orlando was ready with his vision statement and gladly shared it. The man found it fascinating and asked to set up a time to talk because he had a job available for which

Orlando might be the perfect person. The gentleman was a mediator and arbitrator for a union. They got along famously and Orlando found a job that ended up being an excellent fit for him.

It didn't matter to his new employer that Orlando had been out of work for nine months. It was of no concern to him that he had been asked to leave his last job. And, it wasn't relevant to him that Orlando was choosing to change careers. What he perceived was a person who had stepped back to make a conscious choice and who now was passionate and clear about what he had to offer an employer.

Mini-Transition(s) in Spring

As in the previous three phases/seasons, mini-transitions also occur in Spring. These **Exploratory Structures** are opportunities to experiment: to try things on and test them out before fully committing to a particular direction or choice.

Exploratory Structures can take many forms. You may choose to volunteer to gain a personal experience of what it means to work in a field. You might shadow someone for a day or two who has an occupation that you are considering. You can enroll in a class or a certificate/ degree program to advance your learning and enhance your credentials for shifting into a new area.

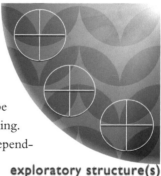

exploratory structure(s)

Think again to the analogy of dating. You can describe the qualities and characteristics of the person you are seeking. Now it's time to immerse yourself in the dating scene. Depending on your style and personality, you may approach this process in different ways. You might comb through a slew of Internet dating sites, or share your list with everyone you know, or begin signing up for classes, workshops, hikes, and events that interest you. Or you may carry out all of the above strategies. You are expending lots of time and energy to find that person that will be right for you. It's fun, it's frustrating, it's tiring, and it's invigorating … sometimes all at the same time.

Each date is a mini Exploratory Structure in Spring. You revisit your vision (mini-Winter), uncover your next date (mini-Spring), commit to a date (mini-Summer), and if you realize this isn't the right person for you, you let go and move on (mini-Fall). If you recognize this is "the one," then you commit in a big way to this new relationship and it evolves into a major Summer.

Moving Toward the Commitment Point

For some, leaving Spring and committing to a new direction can be most challenging. Are you someone who feels comfortable in transition, in your inner world, and at home with the freedom to choose? Are you a creative person who sees myriad possibilities in whatever situation you are engrossed? Do you find it fun to play around with ideas and sometimes find it challenging to settle on a conclusion, result, or next step?

If so, making a commitment and stepping into Summer can be extremely distressing. It means letting go of options. Letting go of options—if that phrase sets your teeth on edge, you must make sure you build as much variety and creativity into your vision as you require.

If you fall more in the camp where you feel most comfortable in structure, then you will experience more anxiety at the end of Fall as you move toward the Ending Point. Stepping into the unknown of Winter and traveling through the creativity and lack of orderliness in Spring might feel overwhelming to you.

Feedback Loop/The Slosh

As Spring unfolds and as you continue to explore the many prospects opening up, you may experience a sort of feedback loop. We like to call this **The Slosh**. That old adage "April showers bring May flowers" is a fitting one, although a bit understated. Instead of just showers, spring is the rainy season in many parts of the world. Thunder and lightning, landslides, and getting stuck in the mud are to be expected.

If you deal with these torrents by getting out your galoshes and umbrella and begin playing in the puddles *a la* Gene Kelly in *Singin' in the Rain*, then you obviously have the energy and clarity to answer the question of "What's out there that fits who I am?" Encountering a decrease in energy along with some frustration and even a bit of anger, indicates that some internal blockages may be arising. It's

> Oh, Spring! I want to go out and feel you and get inspiration. My old things seem dead. I want fresh contacts, more vital searching.
>
> ~Emily Carr

time to revisit Winter and figure out what remains unclear, fearful, or muddy for you. Stepping back to address those internal issues will then enable you to step back out again with new information and more confidence. Winter to Spring, back to Winter and again into Spring, is The Slosh.

Are you an experiential learner? Do you learn and make meaning from your direct experiences? If so, then your Winter and Spring may be a continuous Slosh. To truly understand yourself you have to place yourself in real situations, try them on for size, and then process them internally to figure out their meaning.

Sandy—mentioned earlier in this chapter—would describe herself as having this style. She would say things like "I plan to visit each school I'm interested in. Only when I'm in the actual environment will I be able to tell whether it's the right fit for me."

Maintaining Momentum

While I've touched on some specific activities that are useful in Spring, this chapter will not cover all the available job search/exploration techniques. Many wonderful books are available on this subject. My favorite has always been *What Color is Your Parachute?* by Richard N. Bolles. What I want to underscore is just how crazy and nonlinear this season can be and highlight some additional methods you can add to your repertoire.

As your Spring plan unfolds you will need to maintain momentum and revisit your map periodically to ensure you are headed in the correct direction. Also, you are bound to run into times when you

> The first day of spring is one thing, and the first spring day is another. The difference between them is sometimes as great as a month.
>
> ~Henry Van Dyke

need an additional new perspective or two. You can draw upon many different resources. The following are a variety of "tools" to keep your plan tuned up.

CREATIVITY

Turn your obstacles into creative questions. Instead of thinking "I can't," ask "How can I?" Stay with the questions long enough to find innovative solutions.

BRAINSTORMING

This method helps you break out of conventional ways of thinking to find a multitude of fresh, new ideas. Then sift through all the ideas generated to open up some new possibilities.

SUPPORT AND COMMUNITY

No need to do this alone. Other people can be great resources for new ideas and suggestions, for cheerleading, and for your emotional health.

STRUCTURE AND MORE PLANNING TIME

Make the time to create a regular schedule so that you can keep on track with your plan. If you are not presently working, organizing your time is essential so that the open-endedness of your life doesn't assist you in avoiding the necessary steps toward your vision. Such structuring is just as important if you are working since everything else on your schedule may want to take center stage ahead of your new plan.

RESEARCHING AND NETWORKING

Use these methods to gather additional information. You can then expand your options and make better decisions based on current data.

TRAINING AND EXPERIENCE

You can accumulate lots of practical knowledge and skills by volunteering, taking a workshop or class, interning, or shadowing someone. These are great ways to gather information.

INNER DIRECTION

Carve out time to listen from your "centerpoint." (Revisit Chapter 3 to reinforce this point.) Pay attention to your still, small voice within and the wisdom that is always in and around you. You may be able

Spring has returned. The Earth is like a child that knows poems.

~Rainer Maria Rilke

to listen more closely by noticing your dreams, waking dreams, intuition, and the nudges from inside and out. Other ways to connect with
your inner direction might be through meditation, contemplation, or
prayer.

REFLECTION AND "MOODLING"

Take the time to revisit your vision and allow yourself some positive
free time to let the vision and the plan percolate. You may find jour-
naling, art, movement, or any of your sources of renewal as doorways
into strengthening the vision. "Moodling" is a term coined by Brenda
Ueland in her book, *If You Want to Write.* She says:

> *... the imagination needs moodling—long, inefficient, happy idling,*
> *dawdling and puttering ... the dreamy idleness that children have,*
> *an idleness when you walk alone for a long, long time, or take a long dreamy*
> *time at dressing, or lie in bed at night and thoughts come and go,*
> *or dig in the garden, or drive a car for many hours alone, or play the piano,*
> *or sew, or paint alone.*

> *...With all my heart I tell you and reassure you: at such times*
> *you are being slowly filled and re-charged with warm imagination,*
> *with wonderful, living thoughts.*

AND, REMEMBER ...

Don't ever give up on your dream. There is always a way to create
your heart's vision in the world. Use all the support and resources
available to you. Martha Graham, the dancer and choreographer, said:
"There is only one of you in all of time." Imagine the possibilities!

And Even More Application

By this time I imagine you have a great many thoughts and questions
rolling around in your brain. In the next two chapters let's get even
more specific about how to apply this cyclical approach to your life.

When you are inspired by some great purpose,
some extraordinary project, all your thoughts break their bonds;
your mind transcends limitations, your consciousness expands
in every direction, and you find yourself in a new, great
and wonderful world. Dormant forces, faculties and talents
become alive, and you discover yourself to be a greater person by far
than you ever dreamed yourself to be.

~Patanjali

There is a vitality, a life-force, an energy, a quickening that is translated
through you into action. And because there is only one
of you in all of time, this expression is unique. And if you block it,
it will never exist through any other medium and be lost. The world
will not have it. It is not your business to determine how good it is
nor how valuable nor how it compares with other expressions.
It is your business to keep it yours clearly and directly,
to keep the channel open...whether you choose to take an art class,
keep a journal, record your dreams, dance your story or
live each day from your own creative source.
Above all else, keep the channel open!

~Martha Graham

Where Are You?

THE NEXT STEP IN INTEGRATING the Cycles of Change and making it a useful, practical tool in your life is to apply it directly to your own experiences. I'm sure you have been thinking about your life as you've read about the Cycle, and my story, and other stories of navigating uncertainty. Now it's essential to clarify for yourself where all the major parts of your life fit on the Cycle.

Where Is Your Life on the Cycles of Change?
EXERCISE
Place a dot on the rim of the Cycle that follows to indicate the current position of each main aspect of your life in the change process. Label each dot.

Be sure to include:
- Career and/or job
- Relationship(s)
- Your "Core" (i.e., your relationship with yourself,
  your sense of self)
- Any other areas that are central to your identity
  (e.g., family, creativity, spirituality)

If you are struggling with this exercise, break down major aspects into smaller aspects and feel free to use the following guidelines. They will get you started in placing elements on the left or right sides of the Cycle.

If you are on the Spring/Summer (left) side, then you will have:
- A clear vision for this area.
- Lots of excited (not anxious) energy for it.

where is your *life* on the cycles of change?

If you are on the Fall/Winter (right) side, then you will have:

- A decrease in energy.
- No clear vision for this area of your life.

And, remember, where you are on the Cycle relates to how you *feel*, not what you're *doing*. For example, if you are in a job search but are not clear, enthusiastic, or specific about your longer-term vision, then you would not be in a big Spring. You can still be in a job search, however. Think smaller, transition job while you are still in Winter. You could plot this as follows:

The circle within the larger circle represents a Transition Structure in Winter and the dot in Spring on that mini-transition indicates energy for exploring how to find a short-term financial solution to your basic monetary needs. Feel free to draw mini-transitions within any season if you need them.

Transitions Within Transitions

Life is complicated; there are cycles within cycles within cycles. We can have a vision in any season of the cycle:

- **A vision in Fall** is about letting go or completing something to allow us to step into Winter.
- **A vision in Winter** involves stepping back, healing old wounds, and incorporating renewal into our lives to allow space for uncovering passion and finding a new, alive, next-chapter vision.
- **A vision in Spring** is energized by testing options, trying them on, and exploring the possibilities of the form our vision might take in the world.
- **A vision in Summer** is about committing to launching and building a vision that expresses our uniqueness.

Knowing where we are enables us to ask the pertinent questions and make the appropriate choices for that particular slice of life.

Where Is Your Relationship?

Several years ago I facilitated some workshops for marriage preparatory classes. As these engaged couples were readying themselves for their weddings, they were required to complete a five-week series in order to be married in their church. Each week had a distinct focus including communication skills, spirituality, money, and navigating change. I was thrilled to be asked to facilitate the one on change.

Since the engaged couples were in their 20's and early 30's, they didn't quite understand the purpose of a workshop on change. Of course

where is your *relationship?*

I feel really good about this right now, have a clear sense of direction with it, and feel strongly committed to it.

I'm not really satisfied with this but I'm still trying to make the old way work.

summer fall
spring winter

I know what I want for this area, am exploring the form it will take, and am figuring out ways to make it happen.

I know what I *don't* want for this area but I'm not sure what I *do* want.

they didn't! They were in the honeymoon/beginning of Summer stage of their relationships, still believing that they were going to live happily ever after. The married couples who were part of the team knew better. They loved learning the Natural Cycles as a tool and wished they had known about this concept in their earlier days of marriage. To make the Cycles more relevant to those about to begin their wedded lives together, I focused more on the smaller, nonthreatening changes they were likely experiencing already. Together we

124

explored where the various aspects of their relationships were on the Cycle versus their overall relationships. This next exercise might also help you and your partner to explore what might be in flux in your connection with each other.

Where is Your Relationship on the Cycles of Change?

EXERCISE

Using the descriptions inside the four quadrants at left, think about each aspect of your relationship and plot it on the rim of the circle. The list below is just a beginning; feel free to include additional aspects and eliminate those that don't apply to you.

1. Friendship
2. Level of communication
3. Time spent together
4. Household responsibilities
5. Common leisure activities
6. Romance
7. Family/extended family/in-laws
8. Money issues
9. Sexual relationship
10. Parenting/children
11. Spirituality
12. Dependence/independence balance
13. Place—geographical, home
14. Faith community
15. _____
16. _____
17. _____
18. _____
19. _____
20. _____

how satisfying is your *current work?*

I feel really good about this right now, have a clear sense of direction with it, and feel strongly committed to it.

I'm not really satisfied with this but I'm still trying to make the old way work.

summer fall
spring winter

I know what I want for this area, am exploring the form it will take, and am figuring out ways to make it happen.

I know what I *don't* want for this area but I'm not sure what I *do* want.

How Satisfying Is Your Current Work?

We also can parse our work situation to see what is working and what needs changing. While it might feel as though we want to toss the entire career, if we explore the component parts, we may find that more aspects are still in Summer than we might have originally imagined.

EXERCISE

Using the descriptions inside the four quadrants at left, think about each aspect of your work and plot it on the rim of the circle. Again, the list below is a beginning; feel free to include additional qualities and eliminate those that don't apply to your situation.

1. Personal satisfaction
2. Opportunity for personal growth
3. Supports my life goals and purposes
4. Workplace fit with my values
5. Income satisfaction
6. Interpersonal communication
7. Relationship with boss
8. Stability
9. Effort/Reward ratio
10. Work environment/Culture
11. Challenge
12. Utilization of my greatest strengths
13. Organization-wide communication
14. Relationships with co-workers
15. _____
16. _____
17. _____
18. _____
19. _____
20. _____

By "plotting" ourselves on these maps, we get a better sense of what, in our lives, is most in need of our attention. We become more aware of what is transpiring and, in response, we are able to make choices about how we want to handle the various situations we're encountering.

If you are having difficulty plotting yourself, or if you want to confirm that you have accurately plotted aspects, you can use another approach. Centerpoint has designed a brief, five-question Life/Career Self-Test. It is reprinted here or you can take it online at http://centerpointseattle.org/Start/SelfTest.

Life/Career Self-Test

Begin by choosing one area of your life that is in transition—your career, job, relationship, family, geographic location, or sense of self, for example. Focus on only one area at a time. If more than one area of your life is changing, go back through and complete this test a second time before reviewing what your scoring means. Remember to focus on only one area at a time.

LIFE/CAREER SELF TEST

1. **When I think about this area of my life** ...*(choose one)*
   - ○ **A.** I feel committed.
   - ○ **B.** I am exploring new options.
   - ○ **C.** I am burned out, but I'm still trying to make this work.
   - ○ **D.** I am committed to making a major change or something has forced me to make a major change.

2. **In terms of energy for this area of my life** ...*(choose one)*
   - ○ **A.** I have abundant energy.
   - ○ **B.** I have a lot of energy but don't know where to focus it.
   - ○ **C.** It feels like I'm working harder and harder for the same or fewer results.
   - ○ **D.** I have little or no energy.
   - ○ **E.** I feel new energy stirring below the surface.

3. **About clarity and vision for this area of my life** ...*(choose one)*
   - ○ **A.** I have a clear, specific vision for where I'm going and what I want.
   - ○ **B.** I know the heart of what I want, but not the specific form.
   - ○ **C.** I keep reevaluating and questioning whether this is what I want.
   - ○ **D.** I know what I don't want, but not what I do want next.

4. **When I think about balance for this area of my life** ...*(choose one)*
   - ○ **A.** I am happy with the balance and amount of time spent.
   - ○ **B.** I know the balance I want, and I am exploring ways to make that happen.
   - ○ **C.** I feel like I have no choice about balance; this area exhausts me.
   - ○ **D.** I have let go of the way it has been and definitely want less time focused on this area.

5. **Predominantly, in this area of my life, I feel** ... *(here mark all that apply)*

A.	B.	C.	D.
○ joyful	○ peaceful	○ anxious	○ disillusioned
○ competent	○ confident	○ stressed	○ like I've failed
○ focused	○ playful	○ unhealthy	○ angry
○ passionate	○ excited	○ insecure	○ lonely

Now score your answers:

For each **A** response, give yourself 15 points.

For each **B** response, give yourself 10 points.

For each **C** response, give yourself 1 point.

For each **D** response, give yourself 5 points.

For each **E** response, give yourself 8 points.

A. Total _____

B. Total _____

C. Total _____

D. Total _____

E. Total _____

OVERALL TOTAL POINTS_____

What the Self-Test Scores Mean

30 points or fewer: Fall

You are probably feeling stuck. You're still immersed in this area of life and may be trying hard to make it work but it no longer fits you. You may be getting fewer and fewer results even when you invest more time and energy.

It's time to let go; what you've been trying to make work is no longer working for you. What kind of support do you need to be able to let go, close out this chapter, and create some space to step back?

31 to 60 points: Winter

You are probably stepping back from what you've been doing. You may still be involved in this area but have stopped trying to make it work or you have decided to leave it altogether.

Either way, you probably need time for rest and renewal. Your energy is most likely directed inwardly and, if this transition is a major one, you feel the need to learn more about who you are. This phase is natural. What support do you need to travel through this time?

61 to 110 points: Spring

You have a vision. You know who you are and what you need and are finding new energy stirring to go out and explore how to get it. You must be sure to give yourself enough time to find the right fit for you.

This is the time for networking, researching, and experimenting with new directions. What skills do you need to develop and what resources would be helpful as you take steps to find your best fit?

111 points or more: Summer

This area of your life is going well. You're on track with your vision. You may possibly need a slight course correction or some assistance to better manage your present direction. And, you may want to retake this questionnaire and focus on another area of your life that may be in transition.

Appreciating Our Anchors

You may notice that some important aspects of your life are in Summer or at the Positive Plateau. At the same time, some major components are in the decline of Fall or the depths of Winter. For this we can be grateful. Our Summer anchors give stability and ground us so that we can tackle the profound and often unsettling work of Winter.

"Bill" was counting down the months until he could retire. His job was in Fall, heading toward the Ending Point. His career was in Winter; he was stepping back to think about the next chapter of his life and how he wanted to contribute in a bigger way. One of his anchors during this time was his role as a high school soccer coach, which he adored. It was a life-giving and fun activity for him to support and motivate teens to learn about what commitment means and how to grow beyond their own perceived limits. Another anchor for him was woodworking. He loved coming home from work, going into his shop, and turning wood. In addition to being an anchor for him, it was also a source of renewal, allowing him to refill his well at the end of a draining day.

Valuing Our Challenges

Sometimes, our lives seem to be completely in transition, with every aspect in Fall or Winter. No anchors are at hand; our lives feel adrift in a massive, boundless sea. For this, too, we can be grateful. While not having solid ground under our feet at this point, we do, instead, have the freedom to redirect our lives in an epic way. Nothing external is holding us back from making the enormous changes that we know we have to make.

This doesn't mean that we may not experience some massive internal blockages, however. Stay tuned for the next chapter, which discusses what to do when you feel scared and anxious.

In completing the above exercises, "Joanna" found that her entire life was in Fall and Winter. Her job as a manager of a technical department that interfaced with software users was ending the following year; the company was moving its operations to another part of the world. She was thrilled because she had lost interest in the work a while ago and had been attempting, for several years, to figure out what her next career might be.

At age 45 Joanna attended one of Centerpoint's retreats to give herself an opportunity to access her inner dreams. Now that she was unencumbered by her career, a romantic relationship, and other external obligations, she gave herself permission to excavate deeply to unearth the life that she would be excited to live.

And dream she did. Joanna envisioned a life of travel in Mexico and Central America, photographing people in small villages and championing their efforts in any way she was able. She became determined to live her true values. Because she now had the freedom to choose a simpler way of life, she sold many of her possessions, learned Spanish, acquired some amazing photography equipment, set up a website, picked up her visa, and headed south to live her chosen life.

If her career hadn't vanished out from under her, she might still be working at that same job today. We can easily get trapped by these golden handcuffs: a respectable job, an attractive salary, and other enviable perquisites. But if our hearts are no longer in attaining those external embellishments, it is not only reasonable but also essential to question the role we want them to play in our lives. Simply posing the question doesn't threaten their existence. But not allowing ourselves to delve into our heart-felt needs inevitably cuts down the quality of life we can create.

Not an Easy or Simple Process

I hope by now that you truly embrace the idea that life isn't simple or linear. We can't just say, I'm in Fall or I'm in Winter. We must ask ourselves the question: *What part of my life feels like it's in Fall, in Winter? Or more specifically, What aspect of that part of my life is in that season?*

More than likely, our lives, at any given point in time, are all over the map. It's most probably why we become so addled, confused, and overwhelmed during times of transition. We aren't sure where to focus first so we fixate on one facet that appears to be the most manageable and feasible. That's why work issues tend to be emphasized at the outset and career concerns sometimes become the metaphorical doorway that we must enter to gain an awareness of the more significant problems we need to face.

So then, how can we cope with the complexities of transition?

Working With (Not Against) the Cycles

The privilege of a lifetime is being who you are.
—Joseph Campbell

INEVITABLY, THE SAME QUESTION arises first whenever we share the Natural Cycles of Change: *How long is this going to take?*

How Long Will This Transition Last?

I'm sorry to say there is no hard and fast rule. Instead, I will answer that question with another: *How big is this transition for you?* The correlation is direct: the bigger the transition you are in, the longer it will take.

For nearly 30 years, "Don" had been an upper-level manager in a small, regional company. The business had struggled financially during the recession; they decided to pare back to a bare-bones structure. At 55-years-old, Don found himself downsized. He had been considering retirement for several years, and feeling increasingly uninspired by his work. The layoff was the impetus he needed to think seriously about what he wanted for his next chapter.

Over the years Don and his family had chosen a life of financial frugality. Unlike some of his peers who had lived slightly beyond their means, he had a good retirement nest egg and some freedom to choose when, or even if, he might work again. Don decided to seek the guidance of a career counselor to assist him through this transition.

He had never thought about what he'd be best at. While a senior in college he had heard about this company from a friend who worked there. He felt fortunate to have found a decent-paying position with opportunities for advancement. The concept of passion never even entered the equation at the time.

At this juncture, he was ready to insert some passion into whatever might come next. Don wanted to engage in something that mattered to him and to his community. He believed he was ready to jump into something new, right away.

As we talked it became clear that he identified himself primarily as a person who provided well for his family. His job gave him status in his community. Now that he was no longer employed, Don felt lost and adrift. He thought that the answer to his confusion was to formulate a plan outlining some logical options, yet he had no concrete ideas of what that might entail. He was trying to jump back into Summer. Yet, after a bit more probing, Don admitted that he felt exhausted. Thirty years in a responsible job with many overtime hours had drained him enormously. He needed to answer some essential questions; our conversation sounded a bit like this:

Q. *Does your work vision for the last 30 years still hold your interest?*
A. Not at all. I know I'm done with that career.

Q. *What do you have energy for?*
A. I have to admit, not much. But I should get out there and network.

Q. *You* should *get out there and network?*
A. Yes, I don't want my skills to go stale. Besides, what would I do with myself all day long?

Q. *How does it feel to not have any structure to your life right now?*
A. On the one hand, I like not having to go to a job that I was done with a while ago. On the other hand, I'm a bit isolated. I like having people around. I was good at my job and I got a lot of positive feedback about what I contributed. Now it's just me. I'm going stir-crazy.

Q. *So, Don, who are you apart from being successful in your job? Who are you when you're not that professional person?*
A. I'm a husband. But my wife is still working—she loves her job. She'd work even if she didn't have to work. And she doesn't! You know, I feel like such a slacker when she comes home and asks me what I did during the day.

Q. *I'm hearing that "should" again. You should be accomplishing something tangible that you can point to at the end of the day. Does she expect you to do that too, or is it self-imposed?*
A. Oh, it's all me. She keeps telling me that I deserve to relax.

Q. *But you don't feel that you deserve it?*
A. I just want to figure out what's next.

Q. *And, apart from being a partner, a provider, a professional … who is Don separate from all the other identities in your life?*
A. Hmm, I really can't answer that. My life has always been defined by what I do, not by who I am.

Can you hear how unclear Don is about his vision? He is in Fall trying to take a Quick Fix into a new structure. He is attempting to get away from this confusing, unstructured time. But he lacks energy and has no dream for what he wants. The real challenge for Don at this juncture is how to let go of his past identity and make room for a new vision to emerge. He has to find a way to renew and grow in his sense of himself. Until he does that, the external plan won't appear. Is he ready to enter Winter and explore these personal questions?

And, even more than time, movement is measured in how much we're working *with* the transition versus fighting *against* it or ignoring it.

How Can I Skip Winter?

The next question invariably is: *How can I skip Winter altogether?* That was Don's first thought when confronted with his choices. There is little support for us to be in Winter. How many of us want to feel like we have no direction and have to ask others for support and help? I'm not sure I've ever met anyone who enjoyed feeling lost and vulnerable.

Many of us have either skipped Winter at one point or another or we have seen others avoid it. There is, however, a cost to this choice. On some level you have to shut yourself down and remain in denial. In other words you won't be living a full and mindful life. If, however, you choose to live on a conscious level even when this option is much more challenging, then the simple answer is … you can't skip anything. Just as the seasons unfold, our lives do too.

Learning from Nature's Seasons

Even when someone chooses to live where it appears to be summer all year round, weather variances still occur. For example, in certain parts of Mexico, rain is common from June to October. Conversely, in colder climes, winter isn't the only phase experienced. Once we tune into our natural environment, we can acknowledge the subtle shifts that arise. With climate change we are even more acutely aware of the variations. The northeastern United States is experiencing highs of 60 degrees Fahrenheit in the middle of January. Those differences force us to pay attention day-to-day so we can know whether we need a heavy coat and boots, an umbrella, or warm-weather wear. We watch the Weather Channel thinking it's going to be temperate, but then a surprise cold front arrives from out of nowhere and we find ourselves without enough layers. Conditions can change so rapidly we aren't aware of what we need until we're in the midst of the storm.

In the same way, we need to check in with ourselves each day and gauge our internal thermometer, so to speak. More accurately, I should pluralize the word and say "thermometers." We are not in one place on the cycles at any given time, we are all over the map. Personally I'm on the Equator in my marriage and career—Summer in full bloom—and at the North Pole with my music; I've stepped back into Winter to figure out what I need and want from my singing hobby. Our lives are complex. As we begin to apply this cyclical approach to all aspects of our lives, they become even more so.

Remember, the myth of a linear model is all about "arriving" and "happily ever after." In a cyclical one we focus on growing. It's the journey, not the destination that really matters. We need to try and live each moment as fully as possible.

How Can I Get Through Winter As Quickly As Possible?

A while ago, when facilitating Centerpoint's workshop on The Natural Cycles of Change, we learned something truly fascinating. We had a group of twelve participants, all men whose lives had been driven by success and accomplishment. They were the primary financial providers in their families. In their thirties, forties, and fifties, they had either been laid off from their jobs or were aware that the job choices they had made no longer fit. All were confused and anxious.

After an entire day of learning and applying the Natural Cycles model, they all seemed to reach the same conclusion, one that very much surprised us. They said: "Now we understand ... the goal is to see how long you can stay in Summer and how quickly you can get through the other three seasons. Right?" To our dismay, we thought we had to start over since they appeared not to have grasped a fundamental concept.

While a sort of magnet draws us toward Summer, we can't view Summer as the ultimate goal. Summer has its gifts and its challenges, as does every other season. One isn't better than the others; they are all necessary steps in a growth-filled life.

What's My Core Got to Do With It?

Your core and other parts of your life are correlated. I always think of my core as the part of me who enters into therapy to learn more about myself. In Chapter 8 you plotted yourself on the cycles. Now, take a look back at where you placed your "core" in connection to your "career" or "relationship" or "family" or any other area that is central to your identity. Are they in the same spot or is one leading the other? At times we find that our sense of self, in effect our relationship with our self, needs changing. We have outgrown the life we've been living and, to mature, need to learn more about ourselves in addition to healing any older internal damage we may have experienced along the way. Once we change inside, then we find that the external needs to change to carry on. So we see our career, or relationship, or whatever other key identity we have, become too small for who we are. In other words, internal change precedes the external.

The reverse can also happen. External shifts in identity—we get laid off or leave a job that no longer fits, our last child leaves home, our primary relationship falls apart—can precede internal growth. Our core can no longer remain constant when a big part of our identity is gone. Who am I if I'm not a mother? What's my worth if I can't provide for my family? In a society that values relationships, am I seen as "less than" if I don't have a partner? Something changes outside of us that shakes our very foundation and makes us question ourselves at a basic level.

Going Backward for Clarity

Working with the complexity of the Cycles of Change can at times be confusing. Asking some higher-level questions may be another method for understanding where you are on the cycles. At least they get you in the general vicinity so that you can then probe for more specifics.

Do you have a vision for this area of your life and, connected to that, do you have energy? If you answered yes to both, then you are on the Spring/Summer side of the circle. No clear vision and decreased energy or lack of energy puts you in the Fall/Winter phases, the right-hand side.

It may also be helpful to, in effect, back into where you are by describing the various seasons in reverse:

- If you are in Summer you have made a firm commitment to the form that your vision will take, you are excited about it, and you have lots of energy to launch, build, and grow it. If this doesn't describe what you are experiencing then you can back yourself into Spring.

- In Spring you have a clear vision, a description of what you want, and are exploring the specific form it might take. Energy is available and you find yourself in a creative process uncovering opportunities. If this isn't what you are going through then let's back up into Winter.

- In Winter you know what you don't want but not what you do want. You have said no to the past chapter that has been trapping you, and you have left it, either psychologically or physically. You aren't clear about the parameters of what you need and are spending time stepping back to uncover the vision and learn more about yourself. You do not have a whole lot of energy for being out in the world. If this still isn't the best description of how you feel, then you may be in Fall for this part of your life.

- In Fall you are still in the Life Structure you created but you are feeling trapped, victimized, and stuck. Your energy is waning; you find you have less and less available. You are headed toward leaving this structure on some level, either completely or emotionally, but you haven't made the leap yet.

While you are considering these questions, please remember that you can't consider your entire life at one time. It's essential to break your life identities down into their component parts to understand what each needs apart from the others. The more detail you can uncover, the clearer you will be in working with the uncertainty.

More Helpful Guidelines to Remember

THIS PROCESS IS NORMAL AND NATURAL

Change, transitions, and uncertainty befall everyone, everywhere, throughout the life span. This is normal and natural. Please don't believe those who try to convince you that you can be happy and even-keeled at all times if you could just put your mind to it. Uncertainty, like Fortuna's wheel, can turn on us when we least expect it. If we reframe our perspective and acknowledge that life is unpredictable and at times challenging, then we are more able to make the best choices for ourselves.

During Centerpoint's workshops, countless people have said they knew deep down what they needed to do but they were fighting themselves about moving in that direction. The messages all around us imply that we should keep on that straight and narrow path. Yet, a time comes when we must give ourselves permission to take the steps that we know are right for us.

It's also common to see people who did listen to themselves feel affirmed for the decisions they had made. Even before she arrived at Centerpoint, Leah decided to quit the job that was making her miserable. She knew it was the right thing to do. No one except her partner—not her co-workers, family, or friends—understood how she could toss away a good-paying position. She bravely listened to her gut and took the leap, even before she learned this cyclical map. Something inside us intuitively knows how to navigate these changes. What will it take to give yourself permission to listen to that voice?

BE WHERE YOU ARE

The more time and energy we spend trying to move ahead, or wanting to turn back the clock so we can have it the way it used to be, the more we will feel stuck. The antidote is to accept the situation for what it is and "be where you are," not where you would prefer to be. Running away from the discomfort will not help you move forward. You must embrace the difficulties you encounter and, as the poet Rumi wrote in, *The Guest House,* "Welcome and entertain them all!" Even when difficulties may be thorny and uncomfortable, we have to be open to learning from them.

As we pondered in Chapter 3, you must find your own methods of sourcing your internal wisdom within the uncertainty. Step into your centerpoint to be with what is true and real in the current moment. Sometimes I think there may even be another step here. What if we could not only "be where we are" but also be grateful for the confusion and the ambiguity? How might that shift your outlook?

LISTEN TO ALL YOUR FEELINGS AND NEEDS

From our centerpoint we must pay attention to all our feelings and needs, especially when they seem to be in conflict. In our urgency to uncover the answer and eliminate those annoying, competing voices, we often distance ourselves from the very evidence that will help us resolve the problem. Stay with and listen to these resistant and paradoxical feelings for they contain much insight and understanding.

 **Even If You Forget Everything Else in This Book, Commit These Next Two Guidelines To Memory:**

1) ENERGY IS ALWAYS AVAILABLE FOR THE NEXT, SMALL STEP

As we appreciate the need to be where we are and listen to all our feelings and needs along the way, we can trust that what we have energy for is exactly what will keep us moving in the process. Following the energy will get us where we want to go. I mentioned this as a helpful activity in Winter, yet it applies to all phases of the Cycles of Change.

In my day-to-day work so many things call for my attention

simultaneously; I'm often unsure what to do first. At these junctures I check in with myself and ask: "What do I have energy for right now?" I have to admit that sometimes I'm surprised by the answer! Over time, I have learned to have confidence in my responses.

For example, I had been collaborating with a great team of people who worked with other nonprofits and agencies in the Seattle area. We were developing a consortium, Next Chapter of Puget Sound, to address the needs of aging baby boomers in our region. While I had a pile of to-do's on my list for Centerpoint, I had energy for a task for which I had volunteered for Next Chapter: publishing our website. My rational side kept arguing with me, emphasizing the long list of tasks I needed to complete for my job. But my energy won out and I spent most of the day getting the Next Chapter website live.

And it was exactly what was needed. That afternoon the local newspaper printed an article about our consortium with the web address front and center. We had more than 1,000 hits in that first day alone. If I hadn't listened to myself and what I had energy to do, our consortium would have missed an opportunity to reach many of those people.

Always follow your energy and meet its needs. Don't second-guess what your energy is telling you.

2) YOU CAN'T SKIP ANYTHING

If you ever feel confused, anxious, scared, or overwhelmed, it means you're trying to skip something. You want to have a vision before it's fully formed or you want to know the answer before all of the pieces have been put in place.

Movement happens in small steps; we cannot cross the chasm in one leap or before we are ready. If it's ever overwhelming, confusing, scary, or anxiety provoking, then go back to 1) what you have energy for and take those actions. Trust that they will lead you where you want to go.

APPRECIATE THE WISDOM OF YOUR PAST EXPERIENCES

In the Fall and Winter chapters I asked you to remember times in your life when you've endured transitions and recall how they felt, what gifts you gained, and what helped you successfully move through the process.

People who come to Centerpoint are often suffering what we've labeled *Change Amnesia*. They say things like "I've never done this before and I don't know how to get through it." In fact, if we have a pulse we have been subjected to uncertainty and have lived to talk about it. Even if our past transitions haven't been as earth shattering as the current one(s), we can learn from how we handled ourselves in the past and what has worked for us. Look to those events for hints on how to navigate this current turbulence.

BE OPEN TO SYNCHRONICITY

Stay open to the nudges and signs along the way—those words that you hear repeated from three unrelated people in a day, the lyrics from a song that seem to mesmerize you, that gut/intuitive feeling you get about something. All are important clues to which we must pay attention.

This advice calls to mind a story told at one of Centerpoint's retreats. "Rosa" enrolled because she felt everything in her life was working against her. She had been stuck cycling through the anger and bargaining stages of Fall. Everything was "If only … If only my boss were different, if only my spouse were different, if only my kids were different." During the course of the time away, she came to the profound realization that she wasn't in control of her boss, spouse, or kids or what actions they took. She could only make choices about her own life and behavior. She made the shift into Winter and followed her feelings, needs, and energy. She felt empowered and transformed.

A couple of days later she called us and wanted to tell us about an experience she had as she headed home from the retreat. While driving she found herself replaying that old "if only" record in her head. As she waited for the ferry, Rosa looked up and noticed a sign blinking at her: "Stop. Stop. Stop." She told us she then laughed and remembered all she was able to let go of in Fall, including that way of viewing her life. She could now move on to be with the uncertainty of Winter. What will it take to be open to the synchronicity that nudges at you during your transition?

SEEK OUT HELP AND SUPPORT

First, find ways to create structure in the midst of uncertainty. Design smaller, interim steps to make this transition more manageable. Review all the mini-transitions in each season. Determine where you are and what will be most helpful as you traverse your time between dreams.

Second, there is no reason to "tough this out" all alone. The best way to find the support you need to do this courageous work—and it *is* courageous work, probably the most difficult of our lives—is to ask for it. That may stretch your comfort level way beyond the usual. But you can't just sit back and wait for the help to show up, you have to go and seek it. As you travel this vast strange land of "I don't know," those who have gone before and those who are just beginning to ask the important questions can help you to view yourself with fresh eyes. Going it alone will actually make the work more arduous.

At times our own light goes out and is rekindled by a spark
from another person. Each of us has cause to think with deep gratitude
of those who have lighted the flame within us.
~ Albert Schweitzer, 1875-1965

What if everyone—our families, friends, communities, and countries—truly embraced the idea of a cyclical approach to navigating uncertainty?

10

What If?...

A society whose maturing consists simply of acquiring
more firmly established ways of doing things is headed for the graveyard—
even if it learns to do these things with greater and greater skill.
In the ever-renewing society what matures is a system or framework within
which continuous innovation, renewal and rebirth can occur.
—John W. Gardner, *Self-Renewal: The Individual and the Innovative Society*, 1964

RECOGNIZING OUR LIVES as an opportunity for "continuous innovation, renewal and rebirth" requires us to reframe our perception and question our choices on a regular basis. If you decide to embrace Centerpoint's organic, cyclical approach then it follows that you will begin to see how to apply this perspective to all other parts of your experiences.

> I have been impressed with the urgency of doing. Knowing is not enough; we must apply. Being willing is not enough; we must do.
>
> ~Leonardo da Vinci

What If the Cycles Became a Part of Our Day-to-Day Existence?

We, along with our families, friends, and communities, would recognize the value of stepping back, navigating the time between dreams, and finding sustainable solutions.

Each day we are bombarded with messages about how advancing is more valuable than retreating, action is better than pausing, and that it's not okay to lack direction, or to need help. Yet the reality is that taking the time to thoughtfully develop a new vision leads to greater success and effectiveness in the long run. During this time we, in effect, create a "compass" that helps us navigate the obstacles and times of confusion that are inescapably ahead. We give ourselves permission to step back to uncover new, enthusiastic visions for our subsequent chapters.

When life throws us into chaos, we can now, with intention:

- notice the shift in our energy level
- ask ourselves if our vision is still alive
- pay attention to what we need to end, and
- prepare for stepping back to ask the challenging and, at times, painful questions.

Instead of impatience and that "just do it" pressure, our families and friends would offer the appropriate types of support and encouragement whenever we feel trapped, confused, and adrift. If aware of the cycles, they would be empowered to help and we would feel less judged by them during our time between dreams. We could then choose renewable and sustainable alternatives to construct more healthy lives and communities.

> *Unlike physical progress, which is subject to natural restrictions, the qualities of the mind can be developed limitlessly.*
>
> *~Dalai Lama*

When something isn't working in our modern, consumer-oriented society, the prevailing attitude is that we should simply toss it out and get a new one. Through the lessons we've learned from the environmental movement, we now understand that earthly resources are not limitless. They are finite and we are called to be good stewards of our natural world. As this attitude continues to evolve and spread, let's also consider that the importance of recycling and preservation extends beyond the material. For example, if couples headed for divorce could step back and ponder what in the relationship could be salvaged and healed, perhaps fewer families would unnecessarily break apart. The Cycles of Change model speaks to such essential aspects of relationships and can help couples re-create their connections anew.

What If Employers Grasped the Inevitability of Uncertainty?

We would see improved workplace policies, programs, and systems.

A central theme of this book underscores the fallacy of the linear "climb the ladder at any cost" perspective. It is unsustainable for the long run; it is not feasible to expand and grow forever. And yet, as human beings, we idealize such growth and we delude ourselves and each other that—this time—things will be different. In historical, environmental, and economic terms the cyclical nature of life is obvious. We must now apply this understanding to our workplaces.

Centerpoint's model serves as a "map" for navigating these cycles.

Instead of perceiving employees as "widgets" that are replaced when they wear out or no longer fit, an organic approach allows for the ebb and flow of life to occur. In other words, businesses hire workers who are in Summer with their careers and who are clear and specific about their passion and purpose. Employees who are using their talents and passions in their work are happier, more productive, more likely to make a difference in their work, and their commitment to benefitting the organization is stronger. Employees who are tuned into their skills and strengths are more able to take charge of managing their careers.

When inevitable changes occur in an employee's personal life, e.g., a death, illness, or core transition, the organization would negotiate a new arrangement to adapt to that person's waning energy. The question that then arises is distinct from what it has been in the past: how can the business get what it needs while also meeting the worker's needs, thus creating a mutually beneficial arrangement?

So long as a person is capable of self-renewal they are a living being.

~Henri Frederic Amiel, 1821-1881

Losing an employee means high costs for an employer in unemployment insurance and then recruiting, hiring, and retraining. An organization fares better when it is flexible in dealings with its capable personnel. When the contract no longer fits because the business focus has shifted and/or the worker's vision can no longer be fulfilled in that particular organization, that person would have the freedom to find a new opportunity. The underlying value would be ongoing open and honest communication. No longer could companies hide the transitions and shock their workers by announcing layoffs. And employees would be open about their transitions; they wouldn't leave their manager and colleagues in the lurch by giving just two weeks notice. All would need to be frank about the reality of their respective situations.

These changes are already happening in the work world. As mentioned earlier in the book, one-third of the U.S. workforce is now freelancing. Many people are piecing together multiple part-time/contract experiences to create a life that works for them in terms of balance and finances. The number of contingent workers will only continue to increase. All parties—businesses, employees, government, and policy makers—must address this reality and develop mechanisms that help employees, businesses, and society successfully navigate these transitions.

What If Countries and Governments All Over the Globe Accepted That Better Decisions Are Made With a Cyclical Model in Mind?

I think, possibly, we wouldn't all be in such a hurry to find short-term fixes. We would be more comfortable in that time between and staying with the questions a little longer—and not just any questions, but the correct ones.

One example is U.S. health care reform. It seems that neither side on the issue is satisfied with the outcome. What if our leaders had asked the question: What health policy is best for all the citizens of this country? If we had taken enough time to step back into Winter with this question to find a brand new vision for what's best for everyone, would we have found a different and better solution that works for all? If we had taken into consideration the bigger issues such as the uncertainty of the workplace and the future, would we have been able to come up with a more sound solution to meet the needs of a changing workforce?

I'd like to think that if we had, then our results would have met the needs of more people. Instead of thinking about situations in piecemeal form, what if we looked at the country's and the world's needs as an alive, organic system in which everything is interrelated? In 1964 and still relevant today, John Gardner wrote eloquently about this possibility:

> *Our thinking about growth and decay is dominated by the image*
> *of a single life-span, animal or vegetable. Seedling, full flower, and death …*
> *But for an ever-renewing society, the appropriate image is a total garden,*
> *a balanced aquarium or other ecological system. Some things are being born,*
> *other things are flourishing, still other things are dying—*
> *but the system lives on.*
> *—John W. Gardner,*
> *Self-Renewal: The Individual and the Innovative Society*

What we have before us are some breathtaking opportunities disguised as insoluble problems.

~John Gardner, 1965 speech

Close your eyes for a moment and imagine ...

- Imagine a planet that acknowledges the Natural Cycles of Change—the inherent rhythm of growth and decay—and accepts the interconnectedness of a worldwide human ecosystem.
- Imagine everyone learning from and accepting the inevitable uncertainty and struggles of life.
- Imagine embracing your unique talents, experiences, challenges, strengths, and gifts and choosing a meaningful life that matters to you and to those around you.

I asked you in the introductory chapter if you were ready to live from the "inside out" and learn how to navigate change and uncertainty. I hope this book gave you some tools to do just that so you can continue to pursue the exceptional journey of being you.

To find the way,
close your eyes, listen closely,
and attend with your heart.

~*Anonymous*

RESOURCES

Many diverse authors and writings have influenced this work. As you peruse these resources you will notice that they originate from a wide range of time periods, underscoring the notion that, for eons, people have been struggling with the question of how to navigate uncertainty. Now is the time to integrate the learning of the ages to inject meaning into our twenty-first century lives.

Aurelius, Marcus. "Quotations by Author." *Marcus Aurelius Antoninus 120-180 AD.* <http://www.quotationspage.com/quotes/Marcus_Aurelius_Antoninus/>.

Bell, Janet Cheatham. *Famous Black Quotations*. New York, NY: Warner, 1995.

Bellman, Geoffrey M. *The Consultant's Calling: Bringing Who You Are to What You Do*. San Francisco: Jossey-Bass, 1990.

Boethius, and James J. Buchanan. *The Consolation of Philosophy*. New York: F. Ungar, 1957.

Bolles, Richard Nelson. *What Color Is Your Parachute?: A Practical Manual for Job-hunters and Career-changers*. Berkeley Calif.: Ten Speed, 2013.

Bridges, William. *Transitions: Making Sense of Life's Changes*. 2nd ed. Cambridge, MA: Da Capo, 2004.

Campbell, Joseph, and Bill D. Moyers. *The Power of Myth*. New York: Doubleday, 1988.

Campbell, Joseph, and Diane K. Osbon. *A Joseph Campbell Companion: Reflections on the Art of Living*. New York, NY: HarperCollins, 1991.

Csikszentmihalyi, Mihaly. *Flow: The Psychology of Optimal Experience*. New York: Harper & Row, 1990.

Dylan, Bob. "The Times They Are A-Changin'." *The Official Bob Dylan Site*. <http://www.bobdylan.com/us/songs/times-they-are-changin>.

Freedman, Marc. *Encore: Finding Work That Matters in the Second Half of Life*. New York: PublicAffairs, 2007.

Gardner, John W. "Commencement Address, Sidwell Friends School, Washington, DC, June 13, 1986." *PBS*. <http://www.pbs.org/johngardner/sections/writings_speech_3.html>.

Gardner, John W. *Self-renewal: The Individual and the Innovative Society*. New York: Harper & Row, 1964.

Hudson, Frederic M. *The Adult Years: Mastering the Art of Self-renewal*. San Francisco: Jossey-Bass, 1991.

Jung, C. G., and William McGuire. *Analytical Psychology: Notes of the Seminar given in 1925*. Princeton, NJ: Princeton UP, 1991. 128.

Karpinski, Gloria D. *Where Two Worlds Touch: Spiritual Rites of Passage*. New York: Ballantine, 1990.

Koba, Mark. "Freelance Nation: Slump Spurs Growth of Contract Workers." *CNBC.com*. 3 Apr. 2009. <http://www.cnbc.com/id/29996988/Freelance_Nation_Slump_Spurs_Growth_of_Contract_Workers>.

Kübler-Ross, Elisabeth. *On Death and Dying.* New York: Macmillan, 1969.

Kurzweil, Ray. *The Age of Spiritual Machines: When Computers Exceed Human Intelligence.* New York: Viking, 1999.

Lao Tzu. *Lao Tzu, Tao Te Ching: A Book about the Way and the Power of the Way.* Boston, MA: Shambhala, 1998.

Levinson, Daniel J. *The Seasons of a Man's Life.* New York: Knopf, 1978. Print.

Livingston, Gordon. *Too Soon Old, Too Late Smart: Thirty True Things You Need to Know Now.* New York: Marlowe & Co., 2004.

Marks, Linda. *Living with Vision: Reclaiming the Power of the Heart.* Indianapolis, IN: Knowledge Systems, 1989.

Palmer, Parker J. *Let Your Life Speak: Listening for the Voice of Vocation.* San Francisco: Jossey-Bass, 2000.

Parry, Danaan. *Warriors of the Heart.* Cooperstown, NY, U.S.A.: Sunstone Publications, 1989.

Rogers, Carl R., and Richard Evans Farson. *Active Listening.* Chicago: Industrial Relations Center, the University of Chicago, 1957.

Safian, Robert. "This Is Generation Flux: Meet The Pioneers Of The New (And Chaotic) Frontier Of Business." Fast Company. 9 Jan. 2012. <http://www.fastcompany.com/1802732/generation-flux-meet-pioneers-new-and-chaotic-frontier-business>.

Savickas, Mark L. "Life Design: A Paradigm for Career Intervention in the 21st Century." *Journal of Counseling & Development* 90 (2012): 13-19.

Sheehy, Gail. *Passages: Predictable Crises of Adult Life.* New York: Dutton, 1976.

"Sondheim Guide / Into the Woods." *Sondheim Guide / Into the Woods.* <http://www.sondheimguide.com/woods.html>.

Strayer, Joseph R., and William C. Jordan. *Dictionary of the Middle Ages.* New York: Scribner, 1989.

Thunderbird, Shannon. "Medicine Wheel Teachings." <http://www.shannonthunderbird.com/medicine_wheel_teachings.htm>.

Ueland, Brenda. *If You Want to Write.* St. Paul: Graywolf, 1987.

Yager, Fred. "More Jobs Going to Freelance Workers." *More Jobs Going to Freelance Workers.* 30 Dec. 2009. <http://www.consumeraffairs.com/news04/2010/12/more-jobs-going-to-freelance-workers.html>.

Zohar, Danah, and I. N. Marshall. *SQ: Connecting with Our Spiritual Intelligence.* New York: Bloomsbury, 2000.

INDEX

ACKNOWLEDGMENTS

I am embarrassed to tell you how long it took for this book to see the light of day. Anyone who knows me can tell you that I have been talking about writing this for so many, many years. I am tickled that the work is finally ready; this is an important step in sharing Centerpoint's work with a wider audience to help more people navigate change and uncertainty. In this turbulent world, this skill is more important than ever.

From the bottom of my heart I want to thank my parents, Tom and Roseann Vecchio who have supported this book, Centerpoint, and my career—even when they didn't quite understand what I was doing – through their unyielding love and kind donations over the years. I so appreciate that my 88-year-old father was one of my early readers to make sure that this publication would speak to a variety of generations. Thanks, Dad!

What can I say about Centerpoint Institute for Life and Career Renewal and the many staff and board members who have journeyed in and out of its doors for the past 21 years? Each one of you has given a piece of your heart and care to this work and for that I will always be grateful, even if you may have left on a frustrating, Fall note. It has taken a long time for the world to be ready for Centerpoint's important message; we had to wait until people's lives were in more chaos than they were comfortable with. Please know that your efforts made this book and work possible. My gratitude to you all.

Thank you to the specific board that gave me permission to use Centerpoint's intellectual property, stories, materials, and graphics; I sure hope your dream of reaching millions of folks with this important information is realized. To Leah Krieger who has so competently managed the office as I've been around the country facilitating, speaking, as well as taking the time I needed to finish up this manuscript: I could not have completed this without your Summer enthusiasm and amazing talents. Thank you, Leah.

To all those who have combed through the pages to help me find just the right words and stories to use—Susan Mason-Milks, Dennis Williams, Jan Culp—and to the tens of thousands of Centerpoint clients, past and present, whose stories are contained here in one form or another, I am truly indebted to you. Thank you for allowing me to share your inspiring narratives, even if I did change a few of the details to keep your identities confidential.

Much appreciation goes to my copy editor, Sandy Marvinney, who has a talent for both the big picture and the miniscule details. You've been a solid foundation for me to build upon. I am indebted to Valory Reed of veedot.com, an amazing public relations/marketing person who is so enthusiastically promoting this book and Centerpoint's mission. To Jane Jeszeck of Jigsaw, a whiz at rearranging the seemingly infinite number of puzzle pieces that comprised this manuscript and who designed a beautiful book. Thank you for taking on this project after the former designer bailed and for putting up with my obsessiveness and anxiety. And thanks to Michael Ferreira who took on the heroic task of compiling the index. As a career counselor I believe that when people know and use their natural gifts they can always find a way to make a difference in others' lives. Sandy, Jane, and Michael you have overwhelmingly proven that point! I cannot leave out a special note of indebtedness to Helen Cherullo of MountaineerBooks. org and BraidedRiver.org who connected me with Jane and Michael. You're a lifesaver, Helen!

To all of my mentors and colleagues—there are so many—who have supported and inspired me throughout my life and during my 32 years in the career counseling field: Frank Mangan, Susan Koffman, John Scileppi, Lynne Robbins, John Feerick, Dick Bolles, Bob Reilly, Dave Swanson, Barbara Harper, Rikk Hansen, Mark Savickas, Geoff Bellman, Mike Bisesi, Vickie Chaffin, Karen Shimada, Marc Freedman, and Rich Feller. To my professorial friends, Byron Waller and Heather Zeng, I have so appreciated your perspectives and help in sharing Centerpoint's work in writing, at conferences and in your classes. And much gratitude to my dearest friend, Rhonda Brown; it was fun to get the Spring chapter unstuck on a cruise ship with you. You have all helped shape what was in my heart into something real and meaningful in the world. I am eternally grateful for your belief in me, especially when I doubted myself.

Finally and most importantly, I want to acknowledge my husband, Dennis Williams, who has emotionally supported me through nearly 25 years of my sometimes seemingly crazy yet heart-felt dreams. He has done this by offering both his creative and analytical talents through his incredible photography, the financial management he performs for Centerpoint, and by taking on a yeoman's share of our household chores—including cleaning litter boxes for our menagerie of cats. I am one lucky woman! Knowing that he's on my side has enabled me to achieve this step in my life's work. My never-ending love and thanks, Dennis.

You opened this book to a quote by Williams Bridges about the time between dreams from which this book derived its title. I'd like to end with another inspiring one from John W. Gardner, 1912-2002, U.S. Secretary of Health, Education, and Welfare from 1964-1968, a leader, activist, author, and reformer. This is from a commencement address he gave at Sidwell Friends School in Washington, DC on June 13, 1986. His sentiments are also mine for each and everyone one of you: *I wish you meaning in your life.*

> *...life isn't a mountain that has a summit. Nor is it—as some suppose—*
> *a riddle that has an answer. Nor a game that has a final score.*
> *Life is an endless unfolding, and if we wish it to be, an endless process*
> *of self-discovery, an endless and unpredictable dialogue between our own*
> *potentialities and the life situations in which we find ourselves.*
> *By potentialities I mean not just intellectual gifts but the full range*
> *of one's capacities for learning, sensing, wondering, understanding,*
> *loving and aspiring.*
> *Now, the conventional thing for me to do in closing would be*
> *to wish you success. But success as the world measures it is too easy.*
> *I would like to wish you something that is harder to come by.*
> *I wish you meaning in your life. You are the architect.*
> *Build a structure you'll be proud to live in!*

CAROL A. VECCHIO, recipient of the 2010 National Career Development Association Outstanding Career Practitioner Award, has helped guide people to find their passion and purpose for over 30 years. She is the founder of Centerpoint Institute for Life and Career Renewal, a nonprofit that offers lifelong tools to navigate uncertainty, build meaningful careers, and design courageous lives. A pioneer practitioner in the field of Life Design, Carol is an inspirational speaker and author of numerous articles. She is thrilled that this book will make Centerpoint's life-changing work accessible to a much wider audience. Carol lives in Seattle—a place she truly believes is heaven on earth—where she loves to spend time with her husband, sing *a cappella* harmony, hang out with her cats, design and create jewelry, delight in the outdoors, and take on "urban homesteading" projects.

I wanted a perfect ending.
Now I've learned, the hard way,
that some poems don't rhyme,
and some stories don't have
a clear beginning, middle, and end.
Life is about not knowing,
having to change,
taking the moment
and making the best of it,
without knowing what's going
to happen next.
Delicious Ambiguity.

–Gilda Radner, 1946-1989

CPSIA information can be obtained
at www.ICGtesting.com
Printed in the USA
LVIC061438260413
331146LV00003BA

9780988184800